ASTROLOGY DATING GUIDE

DR. ESRA OZ

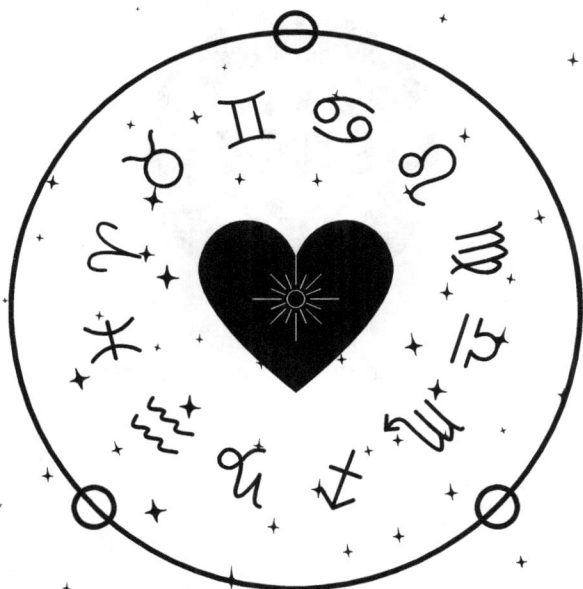

INGI, LLC

Published by: INGI, LLC

www.datingfunnelforwomen.com

ABOUT THE BOOK

Welcome to **Astrology Dating: Guide**, your guide to understanding the deep connections between your zodiac sign and your love life. Whether you're a fiery Aries, a dreamy Pisces, or an analytical Virgo, this book will help you uncover how astrology shapes your romantic experiences, how you attract others, and how you can find lasting compatibility.

Astrology provides a framework for self-awareness and personal growth, helping us to cultivate more meaningful and fulfilling relationships. Whether you're looking for lasting love or just dating for fun, knowing your zodiac and your partner's can bring clarity, improve communication, and enhance your romantic experiences. Love is one of the most complex and beautiful aspects of human experience, and through the lens of astrology, we can deepen our understanding of this powerful emotion and enrich our romantic lives.

This book guides you through the ins and outs of dating by zodiac, offering insights into the love habits, compatibility, and warnings for each sign. Whether you're new to the world of astrology or a seasoned zodiac reader, this is your go-to guide for mastering modern love.

ABOUT THE AUTHOR

Esra Oz, commonly known as Dr. Esra Oz, is an author, coach, and the creator of **datingfunnelforwomen.com**. She is the author of **"Astrology Dating Guide"**. Whether you're a fiery Aries, a dreamy Pisces, or an analytical Virgo, this book will help you uncover how astrology shapes your compatibility. As you explore this book, you'll learn how to spot a partner's zodiac sign by their dating tendencies, how they express affection, and what red flags to watch out for.

You can also join her social media community **"Dating Funnel for Women"** on Facebook and/or Instagram for tips on dating and how to create a dating funnel, a simplistic dating approach, going on multiple dates and filtering out the high-value man, who is offering you the solidity, maturity, and adulthood you need for life partnership.

For more tips on how to date with more intention and less stress, listen to her podcast **"Dating Funnel for Women"** on Spotify and Apple Podcast. She also offers live group coaching on a rotating schedule and 1:1 coaching. Check out the website www.datingfunnelforwomen.com to see when the next session begins, explore the master class, and download a dating funnel blueprint as a reference for your dating journey and follow her on Instagram @dresraoz.

Table of Contents

Chapter 1

Zodiac Compatibility in the World of Apps and Social Media

In the age of dating apps, social media, and rapid-paced relationships, compatibility plays an even greater role. Whether you're just swiping through apps or looking for your soulmate, zodiac insights can help reveal what you truly seek in a partner and how to build a lasting, compatible relationship. Astrology can serve as a unique guide in navigating online profiles and interactions, helping daters understand what signs resonate with them and which traits to look for when scrolling through apps. It can help filter through endless options by offering quick insight into potential compatibility. For example, Scorpio might be drawn to someone with a mysterious, intense online presence, while a Gemini may be intrigued by someone who is witty and active on social media. If you're a Taurus, you might swipe right on someone who appears grounded and consistent, while a Leo would be drawn to profiles that exude confidence and charisma.

Here's how each zodiac sign might approach compatibility on dating apps, social media, and online matchmaking platforms:

Aries (March 21 - April 19): Aries are bold and attracted to profiles that show action, adventure, and energy. They're more likely to swipe right on someone with photos of daring activities or confident, direct bios. They appreciate fast responses and straightforward interactions online.

Taurus (April 20 - May 20): Taurus values stability and might be drawn to profiles that display a calm, grounded energy. They'll appreciate someone who seems genuine, steady, and consistent in their online presence, and might avoid overly flashy or unpredictable profiles.

Gemini (May 21 - June 20): Geminis are drawn to witty, engaging conversations and are likely to swipe right on someone with a clever or humorous bio. They enjoy active users who share updates regularly, keeping things fresh and dynamic on social media or dating platforms.

Cancer (June 21 - July 22): Cancer looks for warmth and emotional depth in an online presence. They'll gravitate toward profiles that exude sincerity and vulnerability. Authenticity is key, and they may avoid those who seem detached or too focused on surface-level interactions.

Leo (July 23 - August 22): Leo is drawn to profiles that radiate confidence, style, and charisma. They'll be attracted to someone who showcases their achievements and looks glamorous or proud in their online presence. Leos love to engage with people who match their vibrant energy.

Virgo (August 23 - September 22): Virgo appreciates clean, organized profiles with thoughtful bios. They're likely to be drawn to someone whose online presence seems well put together and who appears detail-oriented and genuine. Sloppy or careless profiles won't catch their attention.

Libra (September 23 - October 22): Libra seeks beauty, balance, and harmony in online interactions. They'll be attracted to aesthetically pleasing profiles, filled with tasteful photos and well-written bios. Charming and polite messages go a long way with Libra.

Scorpio (October 23 - November 21): Scorpio is drawn to mystery and depth. They're likely to be intrigued by profiles with minimal information that leave them wanting to know more. Scorpios appreciate intensity and will be turned off by anything too superficial or overly revealing upfront.

Sagittarius (November 22 - December 21): Sagittarius loves adventure and will swipe right on profiles that showcase travel, excitement, and fun. They appreciate someone with an open mind and a sense of humor, and are likely to connect with individuals who appear spontaneous and optimistic online.

Capricorn (December 22 - January 19): Capricorn is drawn to profiles that showcase ambition, success, and a strong sense of purpose. They'll appreciate someone who appears reliable and accomplished, steering clear of overly casual or frivolous online presences.

Aquarius (January 20 - February 18): Aquarius enjoys intellectual stimulation and is likely to swipe right on someone with a unique, unconventional online presence. They appreciate profiles that stand out from the crowd and convey individuality and thought-provoking content.

Pisces (February 19 - March 20): Pisces is drawn to compassionate, creative profiles. They'll connect with someone who has an artistic, dreamy, or empathetic vibe online. Profiles that show kindness or a love for the arts are likely to captivate a Pisces.

Chapter 2

Zodiac Love Habits

In astrology, the twelve zodiac signs are grouped into four elements: Fire, Earth, Air, and Water. Each element carries its own approach to love and relationships, influencing the way individuals give and receive affection. Understanding these elemental influences can reveal much about the compatibility and dynamics within a relationship.

Fire Signs (Aries, Leo, Sagittarius)

Fire signs are known for their passion, energy, and enthusiasm. They are expressive lovers who thrive on excitement and adventure. In relationships, they seek partners who can match their intensity and aren't afraid to explore new experiences together. Fire signs tend to express love through action, grand gestures, and emotional warmth. Their love language often includes physical touch, quality time, and acts of passion that ignite the relationship with energy.

Earth Signs (Taurus, Virgo, Capricorn)

Earth signs are grounded, practical, and dependable. They express love through acts of service, physical affection, and building stability within the relationship. For them, love is something that grows slowly but steadily, like a garden. They are likely to show love by creating a secure and comfortable environment for their partner. Their love language often involves acts of service and gift-giving, as they value tangible expressions of affection.

Air Signs (Gemini, Libra, Aquarius)

Air signs are intellectual, communicative, and social. They express love through conversation, shared ideas, and mental stimulation. For Air signs, a strong emotional connection is built on the foundation of mutual understanding and intellectual rapport. They may not be as physically expressive as Fire or Water signs but show their affection through words, thoughtful conversations, and quality time. Their love language often involves verbal affirmations and intellectual engagement.

Water Signs (Cancer, Scorpio, Pisces)

Water signs are deeply emotional, intuitive, and sensitive. They approach love with empathy and seek profound emotional connections with their partners. For Water signs, love is a soulful experience that requires trust, intimacy, and emotional security. They tend to express love through nurturing gestures, deep conversations, and emotional support. Their love language is often centered around physical touch and acts of service that show their care and concern for their partner's emotional well-being.

The Role of Sun Signs in Love

The Sun sign is the most well-known aspect of astrology and represents your core personality, your ego, and how you express yourself to the world. It plays a significant role in how you experience love and relationships. Understanding your Sun sign—and that of your partner—can provide valuable insight into how each of you approaches love.

For example, a fiery Aries may express their love with bold, passionate actions, while a nurturing Cancer will show love through emotional care and protection. By understanding these tendencies, individuals can better appreciate their own love style and that of their partner, which fosters better communication and a deeper connection.

Venus and Mars: The Planets of Love

While the Sun sign reveals your core personality, two other celestial bodies—Venus and Mars—play a crucial role in your love life. Venus represents how we express love, beauty, and affection, while Mars governs our passions, desires, and sexual energy. Together, they shape the romantic dynamics in a relationship.

Venus: The Planet of Love and Attraction

Venus is the planet that governs our love language, how we attract others, and what we value in relationships. The placement of Venus in your astrological chart shows how you express affection and what kind of partner you're drawn to. For example, a person with Venus in Leo may be drawn to bold, dramatic displays of love and may express their affection in larger-than-life ways, while someone with Venus in Pisces might prefer more subtle, romantic gestures.

Mars: The Planet of Passion and Desire

Mars, on the other hand, is the planet of passion, drive, and physical attraction. It influences how we pursue romantic interests and what excites us in love. The placement of Mars in your chart reveals your approach to physical intimacy, desire, and how you assert yourself in relationships. Someone with Mars in Aries may be direct and impulsive in love, seeking excitement and novelty, while Mars in Taurus suggests a slow-burning, sensual approach to passion.

The interplay between Venus and Mars in your chart can provide profound insights into your romantic style, the balance between affection and desire, and how you can best nurture a fulfilling relationship.

The Importance of Moon Signs in Love

While your Sun sign reveals your outward personality, the Moon sign governs your inner emotional world. In relationships, your Moon sign reveals your emotional needs, how you react to love, and what makes you feel safe and secure. The Moon sign is essential for understanding compatibility, as it reflects your core emotional instincts.

For example, someone with a Moon in Cancer may have deep emotional needs for connection and nurturing, while someone with a Moon in Aquarius might prioritize independence and intellectual stimulation in relationships. Understanding your Moon sign can help you recognize your emotional needs in love, allowing you to cultivate healthier, more supportive relationships.

Here's a simplified version of an astrology chart template you can use to map out key astrological signs: Sun sign, Moon sign, Element sign, and Planetary Ruler. **Sun Sign** represents your core identity; **Moon Sign** represents your emotional self and instinctive reactions; **Element:** Each sign falls under one of four elements (Fire, Earth, Air, Water), defining its overall temperament. **Planetary Ruler:** The planet that governs each sign, influencing its characteristics and behavior. The below chart can serve as a guide for mapping astrological influences. For personalized readings, you can input specific moon signs based on birth date, time, and place.

Astrology Chart Template:

Sign	Sun Sign	Moon Sign	Element	Planetary Ruler
Aries	March 21 - April 19	Varies per individual	Fire	Mars
Taurus	April 20 - May 20	Varies per individual	Earth	Venus
Gemini	May 21 - June 20	Varies per individual	Air	Mercury
Cancer	June 21 - July 22	Varies per individual	Water	Moon
Leo	July 23 - August 22	Varies per individual	Fire	Sun
Virgo	August 23 - Sept 22	Varies per individual	Earth	Mercury
Libra	Sept 23 - Oct 22	Varies per individual	Air	Venus
Scorpio	Oct 23 - Nov 21	Varies per individual	Water	Pluto (Mars)
Sagittarius	Nov 22 - Dec 21	Varies per individual	Fire	Jupiter
Capricorn	Dec 22 - Jan 19	Varies per individual	Earth	Saturn
Aquarius	Jan 20 - Feb 18	Varies per individual	Air	Uranus (Saturn)
Pisces	Feb 19 - Mar 20	Varies per individual	Water	Neptune (Jupiter)

Creating a Moon sign chart based on birth time requires precise calculation due to the Moon's fast movement through the zodiac. Here's a simplified template to help you understand how Moon signs can be mapped by birth time. For accurate Moon signs, you'd typically use astrology software or online calculators, but this template provides a basic overview.

The ranges given are approximate. The exact Moon sign depends on the precise birth time and date. For an accurate Moon sign, consult a detailed ephemeris or use an online Moon sign calculator where you can input the exact birth time, date, and location. The template below provides a general idea of how the Moon sign might change throughout the day, but the specific Moon sign requires precise calculation for accuracy.

Moon Sign Chart Template by Birth Time

Birth Time	Moon Sign	Approximate Range
12:00 AM - 2:30 AM	Aries	0° - 15° Aries
2:30 AM - 5:00 AM	Taurus	15° - 30° Aries / 0° - 15° Taurus

Birth Time	Moon Sign	Approximate Range
5:00 AM - 7:30 AM	Gemini	15° - 30° Taurus / 0° - 15° Gemini
7:30 AM - 10:00 AM	Cancer	15° - 30° Gemini / 0° - 15° Cancer
10:00 AM - 12:30 PM	Leo	15° - 30° Cancer / 0° - 15° Leo
12:30 PM - 3:00 PM	Virgo	15° - 30° Leo / 0° - 15° Virgo
3:00 PM - 5:30 PM	Libra	15° - 30° Virgo / 0° - 15° Libra
5:30 PM - 8:00 PM	Scorpio	15° - 30° Libra / 0° - 15° Scorpio
8:00 PM - 10:30 PM	Sagittarius	15° - 30° Scorpio / 0° - 15° Sagittarius
10:30 PM - 1:00 AM	Capricorn	15° - 30° Sagittarius / 0° - 15° Capricorn
1:00 AM - 3:30 AM	Aquarius	15° - 30° Capricorn / 0° - 15° Aquarius
3:30 AM - 6:00 AM	Pisces	15° - 30° Aquarius / 0° - 15° Pisces

Compatibility and Synastry in Love

Astrology also offers tools to explore compatibility between two individuals through a method called synastry. Synastry involves comparing the birth charts of two people to see how their planetary placements interact with one another. This can reveal areas of harmony, potential conflict, and how each person can grow within the relationship.

For example, a couple with compatible Sun signs (e.g., Taurus and Virgo, both Earth signs) may find it easy to understand each other's values and approaches to love. However, if one partner's Moon sign is in an Air sign and the other's is in a Water sign, they may need to work on understanding each other's emotional needs, as these elements approach feelings in different ways.

Ultimately, synastry doesn't guarantee the success or failure of a relationship, but it offers valuable insights into how two people can navigate their differences and build a deeper, more harmonious connection.

A Synastry chart compares the astrological charts of two individuals to understand their compatibility and dynamics in a relationship. It involves overlaying the charts to see how one person's planets interact with the other person's planets. This chart provides a basic overview. For a detailed synastry analysis, you would need to calculate the exact aspects and placements using astrology software or consult a professional astrologer.

The interactions between the planets (aspects) in both charts are crucial for understanding compatibility.

Here's a simplified version of a Synastry chart template:

Synastry Chart Template

Aspect	Person A	Person B	Compatibility Insight
Sun Sign	Sun in Aries	Sun in Libra	Potential for balance and growth; Aries' drive complements Libra's diplomacy.
Moon Sign	Moon in Cancer	Moon in Capricorn	Emotional needs might clash; Cancer seeks emotional security, while Capricorn prefers practicality.
Venus Sign	Venus in Taurus	Venus in Scorpio	Different approaches to love; Taurus values stability, while Scorpio seeks depth and intensity.
Mars Sign	Mars in Gemini	Mars in Virgo	Varied energy styles; Gemini's enthusiasm may clash with Virgo's methodical approach.
Mercury Sign	Mercury in Pisces	Mercury in Sagittarius	Communication styles differ; Pisces' intuition vs. Sagittarius' straightforwardness.
Ascendant (Rising Sign)	Ascendant in Leo	Ascendant in Aquarius	Different self-presentations; Leo's warmth versus Aquarius' detachment.
Sun-Moon Aspect	Sun in Aries conjunct Moon in Cancer	Sun in Libra sextile Moon in Capricorn	Harmonious or challenging emotional expression; Aries' intensity versus Libra's harmony.
Venus-Mars Aspect	Venus in Taurus trine Mars in Gemini	Venus in Scorpio square Mars in Virgo	Potential for sexual compatibility; Taurus's sensuality meets Gemini's playfulness.
Mercury-Moon Aspect	Mercury in Pisces square Moon in Cancer	Mercury in Sagittarius trine Moon in Capricorn	Communication might impact emotional connections; Pisces' subtlety vs. Sagittarius' directness.

Aspect	Person A	Person B	Compatibility Insight
Sun-Sun Aspect	Sun in Aries sextile Sun in Libra	Sun in Libra square Sun in Aries	Balance of individuality and partnership; Aries' drive vs. Libra's diplomacy.

Sun Sign Compatibility reflects core identity and life purpose compatibility. Moon Sign Compatibility indicates emotional connection and instinctual responses. Venus Sign Compatibility shows how love and affection are expressed and received. Mars Sign Compatibility highlights sexual energy and how conflicts are handled. Mercury Sign Compatibility affects communication styles and intellectual connection. Ascendant (Rising Sign) reflects how each person presents themselves and their initial approach to life.

How Each Zodiac Loves

Aries (March 21 – April 19)

> **Love Style:** Bold, passionate, enthusiastic.

> **How They Love:** Aries approaches love with intensity and excitement. They are straightforward and direct, often taking the lead in relationships. Their love is expressed through dynamic gestures, spontaneous adventures, and a fearless attitude. They thrive on excitement and are always eager to dive into new experiences with their partner.

> **Attraction Style:** They're attracted to those who match their energy and enthusiasm. Aries is drawn to partners who are confident, independent, and willing to keep up with their adventurous spirit. They appreciate someone who can challenge them and share their passion for life.

Taurus (April 20 – May 20)

Love Style: Loyal, sensual, patient.

How They Love: Taurus builds slow, steady connections. They are devoted partners who appreciate stability and express love through touch, affection, and creating a sense of security. Their love is demonstrated through consistent care, reliability, and a strong desire to build a comfortable, harmonious relationship.

Attraction Style: They're lured by those who offer comfort, emotional security, and a grounded, dependable presence. Taurus appreciates partners who share their appreciation for life's pleasures and who can provide a stable, nurturing environment.

Gemini (May 21 - June 20)

Love Style: Playful, intellectual, curious.

How They Love: Gemini loves through communication and mental stimulation. They thrive in relationships that offer variety and spontaneity, often keeping things light and fun. They are versatile partners, switching between deep conversations and witty banter, always keeping their partner on their toes.

Attraction Style: They're drawn to those who can match their intellectual curiosity and keep up with their fast-paced lifestyle. A stimulating conversation or a shared sense of humor is the quickest way to their heart.

Cancer (June 21 - July 22)

Love Style: Nurturing, emotional, protective.

How They Love: Cancer loves deeply and wholeheartedly, often putting their partner's needs before their own. They build emotional bonds through care and affection, creating a safe, comforting space in relationships. Their love is expressed through acts of kindness, emotional support, and creating a sense of home.

Attraction Style: They're drawn to those who offer emotional depth and vulnerability. Cancer is lured by partners who make them feel secure and cherished, and who appreciate their nurturing nature.

Leo (July 23 - August 22)

Love Style: Bold, passionate, generous.

How They Love: Leo loves grandly and openly, seeking to create a relationship full of excitement and admiration. They express love through grand gestures, affection, and loyalty, craving both attention and adoration in return. Leo is fiercely protective of their partner and thrives on making them feel special.

Attraction Style: They're lured by those who appreciate their confidence and charisma. Leo is drawn to partners who admire their strengths and are willing to shower them with praise and affection. A partner who makes them feel like the center of their world will win their heart.

Virgo (August 23 - September 22)

Love Style: Practical, attentive, supportive.

How They Love: Virgo loves through actions rather than grand declarations. They focus on the details of their partner's needs and strive to improve their lives with thoughtful gestures and practical support. Their love is expressed through acts of service, problem-solving, and meticulous care, creating a nurturing and dependable relationship.

Attraction Style: They're drawn to those who appreciate their efforts and value their attention to detail. Virgo is lured by partners who recognize and reciprocate their commitment and who show a genuine appreciation for their practical and caring nature.

Libra (September 23 - October 22)

Love Style: Romantic, balanced, harmonious.

How They Love: Libra loves through partnership and diplomacy, seeking to create a relationship that is both beautiful and fair. They thrive on creating a balanced, harmonious connection and express love through thoughtful gestures, charming conversations, and a strong sense of equality. Their focus is on mutual understanding and maintaining a peaceful, loving environment.

Attraction Style: They're drawn to those who appreciate their sense of fairness and who can engage in meaningful, balanced conversations. Libra is lured by partners who value harmony and beauty, and who are willing to collaborate in building a relationship based on mutual respect and shared ideals.

Scorpio (October 23 - November 21)

Love Style: Intense, passionate, committed.

How They Love: Scorpio loves with deep intensity and profound emotion. They seek a connection that is both transformative and deeply meaningful. Their love is expressed through emotional depth, unwavering loyalty, and a magnetic allure. They are fiercely protective of their partner and often seek to explore the most profound aspects of a relationship.

Attraction Style: They're drawn to those who can handle their intensity and who are willing to engage in a deep, emotional connection. Scorpio is lured by partners who are genuine, able to match their depth, and who are not afraid of vulnerability and passion.

Capricorn (December 22 - January 19)

Love Style: Committed, pragmatic, dependable.

How They Love: Capricorn approaches love with seriousness and dedication. They build relationships on a foundation of trust and mutual respect, often prioritizing long-term stability and growth. Their love is expressed through practical support, reliability, and a steady presence, as they work to create a secure and lasting partnership.

Attraction Style: They're drawn to those who are ambitious, responsible, and share their long-term goals. Capricorn is lured by partners who appreciate their efforts, value stability, and are willing to invest in building a future together.

Aquarius (January 20 - February 18)

Love Style: Innovative, independent, intellectually driven.

How They Love: Aquarius approaches love with a sense of curiosity and openness. They value intellectual connections and are drawn to relationships that allow for freedom and individuality. Their love is expressed through unique gestures, stimulating conversations, and a willingness to explore new ideas and perspectives together.

Attraction Style: They're attracted to those who are open-minded, unconventional, and share their enthusiasm for exploring new concepts. Aquarius is lured by partners who respect their need for independence while also engaging in thought-provoking and innovative interactions.

Pisces (February 19 - March 20)

Love Style: Romantic, empathetic, dreamy.

How They Love: Pisces loves with profound emotional depth and sensitivity. They are deeply intuitive and seek a connection that resonates on a spiritual and emotional level. Their love is expressed through tender care, creative gestures, and a strong desire to connect on a soulful plane. They often offer unwavering support and understanding to their partners.

Attraction Style: They're drawn to those who are compassionate, imaginative, and willing to engage in emotional and spiritual exploration. Pisces is lured by partners who appreciate their dreamy nature and who can provide emotional support while sharing their vision of a romantic, idealistic relationship.

Chapter 3

Dating Preferences by Zodiac Sign

Fire, Earth, Air, and Water Elements in Romance

Each zodiac sign belongs to one of the four elements: Fire, Earth, Air, or Water. These elements influence how signs date and what they seek in relationships.

Fire Signs (Aries, Leo, Sagittarius)

How They Date: Fire signs are energetic and passionate in their approach to dating. They thrive on excitement and spontaneity, often leading with bold moves and adventurous plans. They are drawn to dynamic interactions and enjoy relationships that keep them on their toes. Fire signs value partners who can match their high energy and enthusiasm, and they are attracted to those who are willing to take risks and embrace new experiences.

Ideal Date: Fire signs love dates that offer a sense of adventure and thrill. Ideal activities might include:

Outdoor Adventures: Hiking, rock climbing, or a spontaneous road trip.

Social Events: Attending lively parties, concerts, or festivals where they can mingle and enjoy the excitement.

Experiential Dates: Trying out a new sport, taking a dance class, or engaging in competitive activities like a cooking challenge or escape room.

Surprise Plans: Anything that involves a surprise or a spontaneous element, keeping the relationship fresh and full of excitement.

What They Seek in Relationships: Fire signs are looking for a partner who is equally passionate and enthusiastic about life. They value spontaneity and a shared sense of adventure. They seek someone who can keep up with their active lifestyle and is open to trying new things. Emotional intensity and a willingness to engage in bold gestures are key to keeping the relationship vibrant and fulfilling.

Earth Signs (Taurus, Virgo, Capricorn)

How They Date: Earth signs approach dating with a focus on stability, reliability, and practicality. They appreciate the comforts of a well-established routine and are drawn to relationships that offer long-term potential. Their dating style is characterized by thoughtful gestures and a preference for building a solid foundation. They value consistency and find satisfaction in creating and enjoying comfortable, meaningful experiences with their partners.

Ideal Date: Earth signs enjoy dates that offer a blend of comfort and luxury, along with meaningful interactions. Ideal activities might include:

Relaxing Evenings: A cozy night in with a homemade dinner, followed by a movie or board games.

Elegant Outings: Dining at a fine restaurant, attending a wine tasting, or enjoying a theater performance.

Nature Retreats: Visiting a scenic park, having a picnic, or spending time in a serene natural setting.

Cultural Experiences: Exploring a museum, art gallery, or historical site where they can engage in enriching conversations and share experiences.

What They Seek in Relationships: Earth signs are looking for a partner who values stability and is ready to invest in a long-term commitment. They appreciate reliability, loyalty, and a practical approach to life. They seek someone who can offer emotional and physical comfort and who shares their desire for a stable and supportive relationship. Mutual respect and an appreciation for the little things in life are important for maintaining their connection.

Water Signs (Cancer, Scorpio, Pisces)

How They Date: Water signs approach dating with deep emotional sensitivity and a strong desire for meaningful connection. They are guided by intuition and seek partners who resonate with their feelings on a profound level. Water signs often take their time to open up, but once they do, they form bonds that are incredibly nurturing and empathetic. They are drawn to relationships that allow emotional intimacy and vulnerability. Their dating style often involves creating safe spaces where emotions can flow freely, and they value partners who understand their emotional complexities.

Ideal Date: Water signs appreciate dates that foster closeness and emotional connection. Ideal activities might include:

Intimate Gatherings: A quiet dinner at home where they can focus on deep conversations or meaningful exchanges.

Romantic Escapes: A moonlit beach walk, stargazing, or a cozy night by the fireplace with a glass of wine.

Creative Expression: Visiting an art gallery, attending a poetry reading, or doing something artistic like painting together.

Nostalgic Journeys: A visit to a meaningful place, such as where they had a memorable experience or somewhere they feel emotionally connected to.

What They Seek in Relationships: Water signs crave deep emotional bonds and are looking for partners who can engage with them on a soul-deep level. They seek security and trust in a relationship, often placing high value on loyalty, empathy, and emotional availability. Water signs want a partner who will be supportive through emotional highs and lows, someone who understands their need for emotional safety. They thrive in relationships where both partners can be vulnerable, nurturing, and open about their feelings, creating a lasting and emotionally fulfilling connection.

Air Signs (Gemini, Libra, Aquarius)

How They Date: Air signs approach dating with curiosity, intellectual stimulation, and a love for variety. They thrive on mental connection and enjoy engaging in deep conversations, witty banter, and exploring new ideas with their partners. Rather than focusing on routine or tradition, Air signs value spontaneity and adaptability in relationships. They prefer keeping things light-hearted and fun, often seeking a partner who can keep up with their quick minds and changing interests. They are drawn to relationships where communication flows easily and mutual understanding is prioritized.

Ideal Date: Air signs enjoy dates that stimulate their minds and keep them engaged. They seek variety, creativity, and mental stimulation in their experiences. Ideal activities might include:

Interactive Outings: Visiting a science museum, attending a trivia night, or going to a live debate or lecture.

Social Events: A lively gathering with friends, an outdoor festival, or a casual meet-up at a coffee shop or trendy bar.

Creative Endeavors: Taking a pottery class, attending a live theater performance, or exploring art and music together.

Adventure with Conversation: Long walks in the city, spontaneous day trips, or exploring a new neighborhood while chatting about ideas and dreams.

What They Seek in Relationships:
Air signs seek relationships that are mentally stimulating and offer plenty of space for communication and personal freedom. They value intellectual compatibility and are drawn to partners who challenge their thinking and share in their excitement for discovery. While they can be more detached when it comes to emotional matters, Air signs want a partner who understands the importance of open communication, creativity, and flexibility. They appreciate someone who respects their independence but is equally willing to engage in dynamic conversations, ensuring the relationship stays fresh, exciting, and full of new possibilities.

The Ideal Date for Each Sign

Dating Styles and Preferences

Aries (March 21 - April 19)

Dating Style: Adventurous, spontaneous, energetic.

Preferences: Aries loves excitement and is drawn to partners who can keep up with their high energy and zest for life. They enjoy spontaneous dates, thrilling activities, and bold gestures. Routine and predictability can be a turn-off for them. They appreciate confidence and enthusiasm in their partners, as well as a willingness to embark on new adventures.

Taurus (April 20 - May 20)

Dating Style: Sensual, steady, grounded.

Preferences: Taurus values stability and comfort in a relationship. They enjoy cozy, romantic dates and appreciate a partner who is reliable and affectionate. Sensory experiences, such as fine dining or a relaxing evening at home, appeal to them. They prefer slow, deliberate progress in a relationship and are lured by partners who offer emotional security and physical affection.

Gemini (May 21 - June 20)

Dating Style: Fun-loving, communicative, dynamic.

Preferences: Gemini seeks mental stimulation and variety in their dating life. They love engaging conversations and a partner who can match their quick wit and curiosity. They enjoy diverse experiences and are attracted to partners who are adaptable and open to trying new things. Boredom and routine are significant turn-offs for them.

Cancer (June 21 - July 22)

Dating Style: Nurturing, emotional, protective.

Preferences: Cancer values deep emotional connections and is drawn to partners who provide comfort and security. They appreciate thoughtful gestures, such as home-cooked meals or meaningful conversations, and seek a relationship that feels safe and supportive. They are lured by partners who show genuine care and can handle their emotional depth.

Leo (July 23 - August 22)

Dating Style: Charismatic, passionate, generous.

Preferences: Leo enjoys grand gestures and a partner who appreciates their dramatic flair and confidence. They are drawn to those who can make them feel special and adored, and who are willing to engage in playful and enthusiastic interactions. They value admiration and are attracted to partners who can keep the romance exciting and vibrant.

Virgo (August 23 - September 22)

Dating Style: Thoughtful, practical, attentive.

Preferences: Virgo prefers a relationship based on mutual respect and practical support. They appreciate a partner who is reliable and values attention to detail. Thoughtful acts of service and meaningful conversations are important to them. They are drawn to partners who are organized, caring, and willing to work together to build a solid foundation.

Libra (September 23 - October 22)

Dating Style: Romantic, balanced, charming.

Preferences: Libra seeks harmony and beauty in their dating life. They enjoy elegant and balanced dates, such as dinners at sophisticated restaurants or engaging cultural events. They are attracted to partners who value fairness and equality and who can engage in meaningful and balanced conversations. They prefer relationships that foster mutual understanding and aesthetics.

Scorpio (October 23 - November 21)

Dating Style: Intense, passionate, loyal.

Preferences: Scorpio is drawn to deep, transformative connections. They enjoy intense and meaningful dates that allow for emotional exploration. They appreciate a partner who can match their passion and is willing to navigate the complexities of their emotions. They are lured by those who are genuine, confident, and willing to delve into the depths of their relationship.

Sagittarius (November 22 - December 21)

Dating Style: Adventurous, open-minded, spontaneous.

Preferences: Sagittarius values freedom and excitement in a relationship. They enjoy spontaneous trips, outdoor activities, and new experiences. They are attracted to partners who are adventurous, open-minded, and willing to explore the world with them. A sense of fun and the ability to embrace change are crucial for maintaining their interest.

Capricorn (December 22 - January 19)

Dating Style: Serious, committed, practical.

Preferences: Capricorn prefers a relationship built on stability and long-term goals. They appreciate thoughtful and practical gestures, such as planning for the future or discussing career aspirations. They are drawn to partners who are ambitious, responsible, and can offer a sense of security and support. They value dedication and effort in a relationship.

Aquarius (January 20 - February 18)

Dating Style: Innovative, independent, intellectual.

Preferences: Aquarius enjoys relationships that offer intellectual stimulation and freedom. They are attracted to partners who are unconventional, open-minded, and share their enthusiasm for exploring new ideas. They appreciate unique and thoughtful gestures and are drawn to those who respect their need for independence while engaging in stimulating conversations.

Pisces (February 19 - March 20)

Dating Style: Romantic, empathetic, imaginative.

Preferences: Pisces seeks deep emotional connections and is drawn to partners who can engage in creative and spiritual exploration. They appreciate romantic and imaginative dates, such as artistic experiences or quiet, intimate moments. They are lured by partners who show compassion, understanding, and can connect with them on a profound emotional level.

Chapter 4

Zodiac Compatibility: Best Matches and Challenging Pairs

How Each Sign Pairs with Others

Some zodiac pairings seem made for each other, while others require more effort. This chapter dives into the most compatible zodiac matches and those with natural chemistry. This breakdown offers an overview of zodiac compatibility, highlighting both harmonious and challenging pairs.

Zodiac Compatibility: Best Matches

Aries & Sagittarius: The fiery passion of Aries and the adventurous spirit of Sagittarius make this a dynamic and exciting pairing. Both signs thrive on spontaneity and excitement, creating a relationship full of energy and exploration.

Taurus & Virgo: As Earth signs, Taurus and Virgo build strong, stable foundations in relationships. Their practical approaches to life and mutual appreciation for stability and reliability make them a solid match.

Gemini & Aquarius: Gemini and Aquarius share a love for intellectual stimulation and social engagement. Their mutual curiosity and open-mindedness foster a relationship that is both mentally invigorating and full of new experiences.

Cancer & Pisces: Cancer and Pisces connect deeply on an emotional and intuitive level. Their shared sensitivity and nurturing qualities create a supportive and empathetic relationship where both partners feel understood and cared for.

Leo & Libra: Leo's charisma and Libra's charm make for a relationship full of romance and admiration. Both signs value beauty, harmony, and social interaction, creating a balanced and engaging partnership.

Scorpio & Capricorn: Scorpio's intensity and Capricorn's dedication form a powerful and transformative bond. Their combined focus on personal growth and ambition creates a relationship that is both deep and enduring.

Sagittarius & Aquarius: Sagittarius and Aquarius are both free-spirited and adventurous. Their shared love for exploration and unconventional thinking makes for an exciting and forward-thinking relationship.

Taurus & Capricorn: Taurus and Capricorn, both Earth signs, find common ground in their shared values of stability and long-term commitment. Their practical and grounded nature supports a reliable and enduring partnership.

Gemini & Libra: Gemini and Libra are both Air signs, making them naturally compatible. Their mutual love for communication, socializing, and intellectual pursuits fosters a lively and harmonious relationship.

Cancer & Scorpio: Cancer and Scorpio share a profound emotional connection and deep understanding. Their mutual need for security and emotional depth creates a powerful and supportive bond.

Leo & Sagittarius: Leo and Sagittarius, both Fire signs, share an enthusiastic and adventurous approach to life. Their mutual passion and zest for new experiences make for an exhilarating and fun-filled relationship.

Virgo & Pisces: Virgo's practical nature complements Pisces' emotional depth. While they have different approaches to life, their shared desire for meaningful connections creates a relationship that balances practicality with emotional sensitivity.

Challenging Pairs:

Aries & Capricorn: Aries' impulsive nature can clash with Capricorn's cautious and methodical approach. Finding common ground between spontaneity and responsibility can be challenging but also rewarding if both partners are willing to compromise.

Taurus & Aquarius: Taurus' need for stability may conflict with Aquarius' desire for freedom and change. Balancing Taurus' traditional values with Aquarius' unconventional ideas requires patience and understanding from both sides.

Gemini & Pisces: Gemini's analytical and communicative nature can sometimes feel at odds with Pisces' emotional and intuitive approach. Bridging the gap between logic and feelings can be a challenge, but it can also lead to growth and deeper understanding.

Cancer & Aquarius: Cancer's emotional needs may clash with Aquarius' more detached and independent style. Finding a balance between emotional intimacy and personal space requires effort and communication.

Leo & Scorpio: Leo's need for admiration and attention can sometimes conflict with Scorpio's intense and private nature. Navigating differences in emotional expression and personal space can be challenging but can lead to a deeper connection if managed well.

Virgo & Sagittarius: Virgo's focus on details and order may contrast with Sagittarius' love for adventure and spontaneity. Balancing Virgo's practical approach with Sagittarius' desire for excitement requires open-mindedness and compromise.

Libra & Capricorn: Libra's desire for harmony and social engagement may clash with Capricorn's focus on work and structure. Finding common ground between social activities and career goals can be challenging but can also lead to a balanced and fulfilling relationship.

Scorpio & Gemini: Scorpio's intensity and need for deep connection may conflict with Gemini's more light-hearted and intellectually driven approach. Navigating differences in emotional depth and communication styles requires effort and mutual understanding.

Sagittarius & Pisces: Sagittarius' adventurous spirit may sometimes feel at odds with Pisces' dreamy and sensitive nature.

Finding a balance between exploration and emotional security requires open communication and compromise.

Capricorn & Libra: Capricorn's focus on ambition and structure can sometimes clash with Libra's desire for balance and harmony. Balancing career goals with the need for social interaction and partnership requires effort and understanding.

Aquarius & Taurus: Aquarius' unconventional and freedom-loving nature may conflict with Taurus' desire for stability and routine. Bridging the gap between innovation and tradition requires patience and open-mindedness.

Pisces & Virgo: Pisces' emotional and intuitive approach can sometimes feel at odds with Virgo's practical and analytical nature. Finding a balance between sensitivity and practicality requires empathy and compromise.

Exploring Soulmates by Zodiac

The concept of a soulmate—a person with whom you share a deep, natural connection—has fascinated people for centuries. In astrology, the idea of a soulmate goes beyond mere romantic attraction. It is about a profound bond, often believed to transcend time, space, and even lifetimes. Soulmates are seen as individuals who complement and challenge us, helping us grow emotionally and spiritually. In the context of the zodiac, each sign is thought to have particular qualities that resonate with others, creating soulmate-level connections. This chapter explores the astrological idea of soulmates, focusing on how different zodiac signs interact in love, partnership, and personal growth.

Understanding Soulmate Energy in Astrology

In astrology, a soulmate is often someone whose astrological chart complements your own. This might be seen through harmonious Sun, Moon, Venus, or Mars placements, or through powerful synastry aspects, such as conjunctions and trines. Soulmate energy is not necessarily smooth or conflict-free but is marked by mutual understanding, emotional depth, and a feeling of being "home" when with this person.

In astrology, soulmates are not just about romantic attraction—they are about deep emotional and spiritual bonds that help both individuals grow and evolve. By exploring the unique qualities of each zodiac sign and their potential soulmate connections, we can gain insight into what we truly need in a partnership. While astrology doesn't dictate who your soulmate is, it can guide you toward the relationships that offer the most emotional fulfillment and personal growth.

Whether you find your soulmate in a sign that complements or contrasts with your own, the beauty of astrology is in its ability to help us understand ourselves and our relationships on a deeper level. Through the zodiac, we can explore love in all its forms and discover the connections that truly nourish our souls.

While there are no strict rules about which signs are soulmates, certain zodiac signs tend to form especially deep, meaningful connections due to their natural compatibility. Below, we will explore how each sign experiences soulmate relationships and which signs they are most likely to find these powerful connections with.

Fire Signs: Aries, Leo, Sagittarius

Aries (March 21 - April 19)
An Aries soulmate is someone who can match their energy and enthusiasm for life. Aries needs a partner who is equally bold, adventurous, and passionate. They often find soulmate-level connections with fellow Fire signs (Leo, Sagittarius) or with Air signs (Gemini, Aquarius), who fan their flames of excitement. In a soulmate relationship, Aries seeks someone who supports their independence but also provides balance through emotional depth and patience.

Aries Soulmate Signs: Leo, Sagittarius, Gemini, Aquarius

Leo (July 23 - August 22)

Leos seek soulmates who appreciate their generosity, creativity, and desire to be loved. A Leo in a soulmate relationship wants to be admired, supported, and loved with intensity. They tend to find deep connections with fellow Fire signs (Aries, Sagittarius) who understand their passion, or Air signs (Libra, Gemini) who stimulate their minds and creativity. Their soulmate will give them the admiration they crave while also standing as their equal, reflecting Leo's radiant energy back to them.

Leo Soulmate Signs: Aries, Sagittarius, Libra, Gemini

Sagittarius (November 22 - December 21)
A Sagittarius soulmate is someone who shares their love for adventure and freedom. They need a partner who allows them to roam while also creating a sense of emotional security. Fellow Fire signs (Aries, Leo) can match Sagittarius' zest for life, while Air signs (Aquarius, Libra) provide intellectual stimulation and freedom. In a soulmate relationship, Sagittarius will find someone who embraces life's journeys with them, always looking toward the horizon together.

Sagittarius Soulmate Signs: Aries, Leo, Aquarius, Libra

Earth Signs: Taurus, Virgo, Capricorn

Taurus (April 20 - May 20)

Taurus soulmates offer stability, loyalty, and affection. As an Earth sign, Taurus seeks a soulmate relationship rooted in reliability, comfort, and sensuality. Fellow Earth signs (Virgo, Capricorn) understand the Taurus need for security, while Water signs (Cancer, Pisces) provide the emotional depth and nurturing that Taurus craves. A Taurus soulmate will appreciate their need for consistency while adding emotional and spiritual connection.

Taurus Soulmate Signs: Virgo, Capricorn, Cancer, Pisces

Virgo (August 23 - September 22)

Virgos find their soulmates in those who appreciate their attention to detail, practicality, and commitment to improvement. They thrive with partners who value growth, organization, and emotional honesty. Earth signs (Taurus, Capricorn) provide stability, while Water signs (Cancer, Scorpio) offer the emotional connection Virgos sometimes struggle to access on their own. In a soulmate connection, Virgo finds balance between practicality and emotional fulfillment.

Virgo Soulmate Signs: Taurus, Capricorn, Cancer, Scorpio

Capricorn (December 22 - January 19)
Capricorns are drawn to soulmates who share their ambition, discipline, and long-term vision. They need a partner who can support their goals and dreams while also bringing warmth and emotional security into their lives. Fellow Earth signs (Taurus, Virgo) match Capricorn's grounded nature, while Water signs (Pisces, Scorpio) offer emotional depth and intuition. A Capricorn soulmate relationship is often built on mutual respect and a shared desire to build a secure future.

Capricorn Soulmate Signs: Taurus, Virgo, Pisces, Scorpio

Air Signs: Gemini, Libra, Aquarius

Gemini (May 21 - June 20)

A Gemini soulmate is someone who stimulates their mind and shares their curiosity for life. Geminis thrive in relationships where communication flows easily, and their partner can keep up with their constantly shifting interests. Air signs (Libra, Aquarius) provide the intellectual compatibility Geminis need, while Fire signs (Aries, Leo) bring excitement and adventure. A soulmate for Gemini is someone who keeps them engaged, entertained, and inspired.

Gemini Soulmate Signs: Libra, Aquarius, Aries, Leo

Libra (September 23 - October 22)

Libras seek soulmates who value harmony, beauty, and balance. As natural romantics, Libras are drawn to relationships where love is expressed openly and frequently. Fellow Air signs (Gemini, Aquarius) engage Libra's mind, while Fire signs (Leo, Sagittarius) add passion and excitement to the relationship. A Libra soulmate is someone who understands the importance of partnership, cooperation, and mutual respect.

Libra Soulmate Signs: Gemini, Aquarius, Leo, Sagittarius

Aquarius (January 20 - February 18)

Aquarians are drawn to soulmates who respect their individuality and share their vision for the future. They need a partner who can engage them on an intellectual level, offering mental stimulation and emotional freedom. Fellow Air signs (Gemini, Libra) match their intellectual energy, while Fire signs (Aries, Sagittarius) bring adventure and a shared passion for exploring new ideas. A soulmate for Aquarius is someone who appreciates their uniqueness and is willing to explore life's mysteries with them.

Aquarius Soulmate Signs: Gemini, Libra, Aries, Sagittarius

Water Signs: Cancer, Scorpio, Pisces

Cancer (June 21 - July 22)

Cancer soulmates are deeply connected on an emotional level. As one of the most nurturing signs, Cancer seeks a partner who values emotional intimacy, security, and home. Water signs (Scorpio, Pisces) provide the depth of feeling Cancer craves, while Earth signs (Taurus, Virgo) offer the stability and comfort Cancer needs. A Cancer soulmate is someone who offers love, protection, and a deep emotional bond.

Cancer Soulmate Signs: Scorpio, Pisces, Taurus, Virgo

Scorpio (October 23 - November 21)

Scorpios seek soulmates who can match their intensity, passion, and emotional depth. They thrive in relationships where trust, loyalty, and transformation are key themes. Water signs (Cancer, Pisces) understand Scorpio's emotional complexity, while Earth signs (Virgo, Capricorn) offer groundedness and loyalty. A Scorpio soulmate will engage them in deep emotional and spiritual growth, creating a connection that transcends the ordinary.

Scorpio Soulmate Signs: Cancer, Pisces, Virgo, Capricorn

Pisces (February 19 - March 20)

Pisces are drawn to soulmates who offer emotional depth, compassion, and spiritual connection. As a highly intuitive and romantic sign, Pisces seek partners who can connect with them on a soul level. Water signs (Cancer, Scorpio) provide emotional understanding, while Earth signs (Taurus, Capricorn) offer stability and support. A Pisces soulmate will share their dreams and help them feel grounded in reality, all while fostering a deep, soulful connection.

Pisces Soulmate Signs: Cancer, Scorpio, Taurus, Capricorn

Chapter 5

The Lure of Each Zodiac: How They Draw You In

Every zodiac has a unique way of attracting others. Understanding how each sign lures potential partners can help you see through the charm (or mystery) and know what to expect.

Aries (March 21 – April 19): Aries attracts with boldness and passion. They approach love with intensity and excitement, often taking the lead in relationships. Their dynamic gestures and spontaneous nature make them thrilling partners who are always eager to dive into new experiences.

Taurus (April 20 – May 20): Taurus builds connections slowly and steadily. They are devoted, loyal partners who appreciate stability and express love through touch and affection. Their allure lies in their consistency and ability to create a comfortable, harmonious environment.

Gemini (May 21 – June 20): Geminis are the ultimate conversationalists. They pull you in with their wit, intellectual curiosity, and lively charm. Their easy adaptability makes you feel like they're the perfect partner for any occasion. They keep things fresh and engaging with their ever-changing interests and ideas.

Cancer (June 21 – July 22): Cancer loves deeply and wholeheartedly, often putting their partner's needs before their own. They build emotional bonds through care and affection, creating a safe, comforting space in relationships. Their nurturing, protective nature draws people in who seek emotional depth and security.

Leo (July 23 – August 22): Leos attract with their magnetic charisma and confidence. They radiate warmth and enthusiasm, often taking center stage and drawing others in with their vibrant personality. Their love is grand and generous, making their partners feel special and adored.

Virgo (August 23 – September 22): Virgos captivate with their meticulous attention to detail and practical approach. They are drawn to those who appreciate their thoughtfulness and precision. Their love is expressed through acts of service and a deep commitment to improving and nurturing their relationship.

Libra (September 23 – October 22): Libras charm with their grace and diplomatic nature. They are skilled at creating harmony and balance, making them attractive to those who value partnership and cooperation. Their love is expressed through elegance, fairness, and a desire for mutual understanding.

Scorpio (October 23 – November 21): Scorpios lure you in with intensity. Their enigmatic presence and deep passion make you feel like you're the only person in the room. However, they don't reveal everything at once, creating an air of mystery and intrigue that keeps you coming back for more.

Sagittarius (November 22 – December 21): Sagittarians attract with their adventurous spirit and optimism. They are drawn to those who share their love for exploration and new experiences. Their love is expressed through freedom, excitement, and a desire to discover the world together.

Capricorn (December 22 – January 19): Capricorns allure with their ambition and determination. They attract those who appreciate their drive and reliability. Their love is expressed through practical support, commitment, and a steady, dependable presence.

Aquarius (January 20 – February 18): Aquarians captivate with their originality and intellect. They are drawn to those who embrace their unique perspectives and innovative ideas. Their love is expressed through intellectual stimulation, open-mindedness, and a deep appreciation for individuality.

Pisces (February 19 – March 20): Pisces draw you in with their empathy and creativity. They have a way of making you feel understood and cherished, often through their artistic expression and emotional depth. Their love is tender, imaginative, and deeply compassionate.

Chapter 6

Warnings Based on Zodiac Traits

Sometimes love comes with warning signs. Here's what you should watch out for when dating each zodiac.

Aries (March 21 – April 19)

> **Warning**: Aries' intensity and spontaneity can sometimes come across as impulsive or reckless. Their desire for excitement might lead to a lack of stability in the relationship.

> **Red Flag**: Watch out for a tendency to prioritize their own needs and desires over the relationship. Their assertiveness can sometimes turn into aggression if they feel challenged or restricted.

Taurus (April 20 – May 20)

> **Warning**: Taurus values stability and comfort, which can sometimes translate into stubbornness or resistance to change. They may struggle with adapting to new situations or perspectives.

> **Red Flag**: Be cautious of possessiveness or an overly materialistic attitude. Taurus may have difficulty letting go of control or accepting change, which can create tension in the relationship.

Gemini (May 21 – June 20)

> **Warning**: Geminis' need for variety and intellectual stimulation can sometimes lead to inconsistency or a lack of commitment. Their dual nature might cause them to seem unpredictable.

> **Red Flag**: Watch for signs of superficiality or an inability to focus on one person or situation for too long. Their tendency to change their mind frequently can lead to confusion and frustration.

Cancer (June 21 – July 22)

Warning: Cancer's emotional depth can sometimes make them overly sensitive or moody. Their strong need for security might lead to clinginess or insecurity in the relationship.

Red Flag: Be wary of excessive dependency or emotional manipulation. Cancer's protective nature can sometimes result in controlling behaviors if they feel threatened.

Leo (July 23 – August 22)

Warning: Leos' confidence and need for admiration can sometimes come across as arrogance or self-centeredness. Their desire to be in the spotlight might overshadow their partner's needs.

Red Flag: Watch out for a tendency to dominate conversations or demand excessive attention. Their dramatic nature might lead to conflicts if they feel unappreciated or overshadowed.

Virgo (August 23 – September 22)

Warning: Virgos' attention to detail and perfectionism can sometimes make them overly critical or nitpicky. Their desire for order and structure might create tension if their partner is more laid-back.

Red Flag: Be cautious of excessive criticism or a tendency to focus on flaws rather than positives. Their need for control and perfection might lead to unrealistic expectations.

Libra (September 23 – October 22)

Warning: Libras' desire for harmony and balance can sometimes lead to indecisiveness or a lack of assertiveness. They may struggle with making firm decisions or standing up for themselves.

Red Flag: Watch for signs of people-pleasing behavior or difficulty expressing their true feelings. Their tendency to avoid conflict might result in unresolved issues or dissatisfaction.

Scorpio (October 23 – November 21)

Warning: Scorpios' intensity and passion can sometimes lead to jealousy or possessiveness. Their deep emotional nature might make them prone to dramatic reactions or secrecy.

Red Flag: Be cautious of manipulative behavior or an unwillingness to communicate openly. Their need for control and deep emotional involvement can sometimes be overwhelming.

Sagittarius (November 22 – December 21)

Warning: Sagittarians' love for freedom and adventure can sometimes result in restlessness or a fear of commitment. Their desire for new experiences might lead to inconsistency in the relationship.

Red Flag: Watch for a tendency to be overly blunt or insensitive. Their need for independence might lead to neglect of the relationship's emotional needs.

Capricorn (December 22 – January 19)

Warning: Capricorns can be intensely focused on their goals. While they are committed partners, their ambition can sometimes take priority over romance, leaving their partner feeling neglected.

Red Flag: Be wary of their tendency to prioritize work or personal achievements over relationship matters. Their seriousness and dedication might make them appear emotionally distant.

Aquarius (January 20 – February 18)

>**Warning**: Aquarians' need for independence and unconventional thinking can sometimes make them seem detached or aloof. Their focus on ideals might overshadow personal connection.

>**Red Flag**: Watch out for emotional detachment or a lack of commitment to the relationship. Their tendency to prioritize their own interests or ideas can lead to feelings of neglect.

Pisces (February 19 – March 20)

>**Warning**: Pisces are dreamers, but sometimes they get lost in fantasy. They may struggle with practical issues or face difficulty maintaining boundaries in relationships.

>**Red Flag**: Be cautious of emotional unavailability or a tendency to idealize relationships beyond what's realistic. Their escapist tendencies might lead to misunderstandings or disappointment.

Understanding Toxic Patterns for Each Zodiac Sign

While each zodiac sign has its strengths and gifts in love, there are also potential toxic patterns that can emerge, especially when they are out of balance. Understanding the toxic patterns of each zodiac sign can help us recognize areas for growth and self-improvement. These tendencies are not fixed but can be overcome through self-awareness, empathy, and communication. By acknowledging and addressing these toxic behaviors, we can cultivate healthier, more fulfilling relationships with ourselves and others. Each zodiac sign has the potential for deep connection and love, as long as we are willing to confront and heal the patterns that hold us back. Understanding these patterns is crucial for personal growth and building healthier relationships. Here, we explore the toxic tendencies of each sign and how they can manifest in relationships.

Fire Signs: Aries, Leo, Sagittarius

Aries (March 21 - April 19)

Toxic Pattern: Impulsiveness and Aggression

Aries is known for their fiery and assertive nature, but when this energy becomes unbalanced, it can manifest as impulsiveness and aggression. In relationships, Aries can become too demanding, easily frustrated, and prone to selfishness. Their need to act without thinking can lead to rash decisions or arguments, creating conflict where patience and understanding are needed.

How to Overcome: Aries should focus on developing patience and practicing empathy, ensuring they consider their partner's feelings before acting or reacting.

Leo (July 23 - August 22)

Toxic Pattern: Arrogance and Attention-Seeking

Leo thrives in the spotlight, but their need for attention can turn toxic when it leads to arrogance and selfish behavior. In relationships, Leo might become too focused on their own needs, expecting constant admiration and validation without reciprocating. This self-centeredness can make their partner feel overlooked or unappreciated.

How to Overcome: Leo should practice humility and learn to share the spotlight, appreciating their partner's needs and contributions to the relationship.

Sagittarius (November 22 - December 21)

Toxic Pattern: Commitment Avoidance and Restlessness

Sagittarius loves freedom and adventure, but this can manifest as a fear of commitment or a tendency to avoid responsibility in relationships. Their need for independence can lead them to distance themselves emotionally or even physically when things get too serious. This restlessness can leave their partner feeling uncertain about the future.

How to Overcome: Sagittarius should work on finding a balance between independence and commitment, learning to invest emotionally without feeling trapped.

Earth Signs: Taurus, Virgo, Capricorn

Taurus (April 20 - May 20)

Toxic Pattern: Stubbornness and Possessiveness

Taurus values stability and security, but this can become toxic when they become overly stubborn or possessive. In relationships, they may resist change or be inflexible, demanding control over situations or their partner. Their possessiveness can make their partner feel suffocated or restricted, leading to tension and frustration.

How to Overcome: Taurus should practice flexibility and trust, allowing space for their partner's individuality and embracing change as a natural part of growth.

Virgo (August 23 - September 22)

Toxic Pattern: Perfectionism and Criticism

Virgo's attention to detail is a strength, but it can become toxic when it leads to constant criticism or unrealistic expectations. In relationships, Virgo may become overly judgmental or focus on their partner's flaws, striving for a level of perfection that is impossible to achieve. This can create feelings of inadequacy and resentment in their partner.

How to Overcome: Virgo should focus on accepting imperfections, both in themselves and others, and practice offering support and understanding instead of criticism.

Capricorn (December 22 - January 19)

Toxic Pattern: Workaholism and Emotional Distance

Capricorns are ambitious and driven, but their focus on success can become toxic when it leads to workaholism or emotional neglect in relationships. They may prioritize their career or goals over their partner, becoming distant or detached. This emotional coldness can leave their partner feeling unsupported or undervalued.

How to Overcome: Capricorn should work on balancing their professional and personal life, making time for emotional intimacy and showing their partner they are valued.

Air Signs: Gemini, Libra, Aquarius

Gemini (May 21 - June 20)

Toxic Pattern: Inconsistency and Indecisiveness

Gemini's adaptability can turn toxic when it leads to inconsistency or a lack of commitment. In relationships, they may change their mind frequently or struggle to make decisions, leaving their partner feeling uncertain or confused. Their tendency to be distracted or noncommittal can make it difficult to build a stable relationship.

How to Overcome: Gemini should focus on being more decisive and consistent in their actions, offering stability and clarity to their partner.

Libra (September 23 - October 22)

Toxic Pattern: People-Pleasing and Avoiding Conflict

Libras value harmony, but their desire to avoid conflict can become toxic when it leads to people-pleasing or dishonesty. In relationships, Libra may sacrifice their own needs or opinions to keep the peace, which can lead to resentment or passive-aggressive behavior. Their fear of confrontation can prevent issues from being resolved, leading to long-term dissatisfaction.

How to Overcome: Libra should learn to embrace conflict as a necessary part of growth, expressing their true feelings and standing up for their needs.

Aquarius (January 20 - February 18)

Toxic Pattern: Emotional Detachment and Aloofness

Aquarius values independence and intellect, but this can become toxic when they detach emotionally or become too aloof. In relationships, Aquarius may struggle to connect on a deeper emotional level, preferring to keep things light or distant. Their tendency to intellectualize emotions can make their partner feel misunderstood or unloved.

How to Overcome: Aquarius should work on being more emotionally present, allowing themselves to be vulnerable and creating deeper emotional intimacy with their partner.

Water Signs: Cancer, Scorpio, Pisces

Cancer (June 21 - July 22)

Toxic Pattern: Clinginess and Over-Sensitivity

Cancer's deep emotional connection can turn toxic when they become overly clingy or dependent in relationships. Their fear of abandonment may lead them to smother their partner or demand constant reassurance. Cancers can also be extremely sensitive, taking things too personally or becoming overly reactive to perceived slights.

How to Overcome: Cancer should practice emotional independence, learning to trust in their partner's love without needing constant validation.

Scorpio (October 23 - November 21)

Toxic Pattern: Jealousy and Control

Scorpio's intensity in love can become toxic when it turns into jealousy or control. In relationships, they may become possessive or suspicious, struggling to trust their partner fully. Their need for control can create power struggles, as they may attempt to dominate or manipulate the relationship to feel secure.

How to Overcome: Scorpio should focus on building trust and allowing their partner the freedom to grow, practicing vulnerability instead of control.

Pisces (February 19 - March 20)

Toxic Pattern: Escapism and Victim Mentality

Pisces' dreamy and compassionate nature can turn toxic when they avoid facing reality or fall into a victim mindset. In relationships, they may retreat into their own world to escape conflict or become overly passive, expecting their partner to solve their problems. Their tendency to idealize relationships can lead to disappointment when reality doesn't match their fantasies.

How to Overcome: Pisces should work on grounding themselves in reality, taking responsibility for their actions, and addressing issues head-on instead of avoiding them.

Chapter 7

Zodiac Couples: Power Matches and Challenges

Some zodiac pairings create power couples who complement each other's strengths, while others may face challenges. Here's a deeper look into some pairings:

Aries & Libra: Aries' boldness and enthusiasm are balanced by Libra's charm and diplomacy. This pairing thrives on mutual admiration and balancing each other's desires for excitement and harmony. They need to work on compromising, as Aries' impulsiveness and Libra's indecision can create friction.

Taurus & Scorpio: Taurus' reliability and sensuality complement Scorpio's intensity and passion. Both value loyalty and depth, which can lead to a powerful, transformative relationship. They need to navigate Taurus' stubbornness and Scorpio's possessiveness to maintain harmony.

Gemini & Sagittarius: Gemini's curiosity and versatility are perfectly matched by Sagittarius's adventurous spirit and optimism. Both love exploration and intellectual stimulation, making them an exciting and dynamic couple. They need to manage their mutual restlessness and tendency to avoid routine.

Cancer & Capricorn: Cancer's nurturing and emotional depth blend well with Capricorn's practicality and ambition. They provide each other with emotional security and stability. Their challenge lies in balancing Cancer's need for emotional expression with Capricorn's reserved nature.

Leo & Aquarius: Both bold in their own ways, Leo and Aquarius can become an unstoppable duo. Leo's charisma balances Aquarius's unique, independent thinking, creating a relationship full of mutual admiration.

They need to avoid clashes over control, as Leo's need for attention can conflict with Aquarius's desire for freedom.

Virgo & Pisces: Virgo's practicality and attention to detail harmonize with Pisces's creativity and emotional depth. They can create a deeply supportive and understanding relationship. Their challenge lies in managing Virgo's critical nature and Pisces's tendency to escape from reality.

Aries & Capricorn: Aries' dynamic energy and ambition complement Capricorn's disciplined, goal-oriented approach. This pairing can achieve great things together. They need to avoid conflicts over Aries' impulsiveness and Capricorn's cautious nature to maintain balance.

Taurus & Libra: Taurus's sensuality and stability are well-matched with Libra's charm and need for balance. They can create a harmonious and aesthetically pleasing relationship. Their challenge lies in managing Taurus's possessiveness and Libra's indecision.

Gemini & Virgo: Gemini's versatility and intellectual curiosity pair well with Virgo's attention to detail and practicality. They can stimulate each other intellectually and creatively. Their challenge is to manage Gemini's inconsistency and Virgo's perfectionism.

Cancer & Pisces: Both water signs, Cancer and Pisces share a deep emotional connection and intuitive understanding. They can create a nurturing and supportive relationship. Their challenge is to avoid getting lost in their emotional worlds and ensure they maintain practical aspects of the relationship.

Leo & Sagittarius: Leo's confidence and passion are well-matched with Sagittarius's adventurous spirit and optimism. They can create an exciting and dynamic relationship full of shared enthusiasm. Their challenge is to manage Leo's need for attention and Sagittarius's fear of commitment.

Virgo & Capricorn: Both earth signs, Virgo and Capricorn share a practical and disciplined approach to life. They can create a stable and productive relationship. Their challenge is to manage Virgo's critical nature and Capricorn's tendency to be emotionally reserved.

Aquarius & Gemini: Aquarius's originality and Gemini's versatility create a relationship full of intellectual stimulation and excitement. They thrive on each other's curiosity and adaptability. Their challenge is to avoid becoming too detached or scattered in their focus.

Pisces & Scorpio: Pisces's emotional depth and Scorpio's intensity create a powerful and transformative relationship. They connect on a deep emotional level and support each other's growth. Their challenge is to manage Scorpio's possessiveness and Pisces's tendency to idealize.

Aries & Sagittarius: Both fire signs, Aries and Sagittarius share a love for adventure and excitement. They can create an energetic and passionate relationship. Their challenge is to manage their mutual restlessness and tendency to avoid routine.

Taurus & Aquarius: Taurus's need for stability and comfort contrasts with Aquarius's desire for freedom and innovation. They can complement each other's strengths but need to work on reconciling Taurus's need for security with Aquarius's need for independence.

Gemini & Pisces: Gemini's versatility and Pisces's creativity create a relationship full of imaginative and stimulating experiences. They need to manage Gemini's inconsistency and Pisces's tendency to get lost in fantasy.

Cancer & Leo: Cancer's nurturing and emotional depth complement Leo's confidence and enthusiasm. They can create a supportive and dynamic relationship. Their challenge lies in balancing Cancer's need for emotional security with Leo's need for admiration and attention.

Virgo & Libra: Virgo's practicality and attention to detail balance Libra's charm and desire for harmony. They can create a balanced and aesthetically pleasing relationship. Their challenge is to manage Virgo's critical nature and Libra's indecision.

Scorpio & Aquarius: Scorpio's intensity and passion contrast with Aquarius's detached and unconventional nature. They can create a dynamic and transformative relationship but need to work on reconciling Scorpio's need for emotional depth with Aquarius's desire for independence.

Sagittarius & Capricorn: Sagittarius's adventurous spirit and optimism contrast with Capricorn's practicality and ambition. They can complement each other's strengths but need to manage Sagittarius's need for freedom with Capricorn's focus on goals and stability.

Aquarius & Pisces: Aquarius's originality and Pisces's emotional depth create a relationship full of imaginative and compassionate experiences. Their challenge is to manage Aquarius's detachment and Pisces's tendency to idealize.

Chapter 8

Navigating Breakups by Zodiac

Breakups can be tough, but understanding your zodiac's approach to heartache can make the healing process smoother.

Aries (March 21 – April 19): Aries may react to a breakup with intense emotions and a desire to move on quickly. Their impulsive nature can lead them to jump into new activities or relationships as a way to distract themselves. They need to be mindful of not rushing their healing process and taking the time to reflect on the end of the relationship.

Taurus (April 20 – May 20): Taurus processes breakups slowly and methodically. They value stability and may struggle with the change, often taking time to adjust and find new routines. They might seek comfort in familiar places and people. It's important for them to allow themselves time to grieve and not rush into new commitments.

Gemini (May 21 – June 20): Geminis tend to use their intellectual curiosity to analyze the breakup from all angles. They may talk about their feelings with friends or seek new social interactions to distract themselves. They need to make sure they're not avoiding their emotions and allow themselves to feel and heal.

Cancer (June 21 – July 22): Cancer is deeply affected by breakups and may retreat into their shell to process their emotions. They often need to nurture themselves and seek support from close friends and family. It's essential for them to acknowledge and express their feelings rather than bottling them up.

Leo (July 23 – August 22): Leos hate rejection, and a breakup can deeply wound their pride. They'll likely focus on regaining their confidence and may seek validation from others during the healing process. They need to work on self-love and avoiding superficial distractions and allow themselves to genuinely process the end of the relationship.

Virgo (August 23 – September 22): Virgos tend to analyze the breakup in detail, often reflecting on what went wrong and what they could have done differently. Their practical approach can help them find closure, but they need to be careful not to overanalyze or blame themselves excessively. It's important for them to take care of their emotional well-being and not just focus on practical solutions.

Libra (September 23 – October 22): Libras may struggle with a breakup due to their desire for harmony and balance. They often seek to maintain peace and may avoid confronting the full impact of the breakup. They need to allow themselves to fully experience their emotions and not just focus on maintaining a facade of calm.

Scorpio (October 23 – November 21): Scorpios experience breakups intensely and may go through a period of deep emotional introspection. They might keep their feelings private and need time to heal on their own terms. It's important for them to confront their emotions and avoid falling into destructive patterns or isolating themselves.

Sagittarius (November 22 – December 21): Sagittarians may initially respond to a breakup by seeking new adventures or distractions. They often use their optimism and enthusiasm to move on quickly. They need to make sure they're not avoiding their feelings and take the time to process the end of the relationship before fully diving into new pursuits.

Capricorn (December 22 – January 19): Capricorns may approach a breakup with a pragmatic mindset, focusing on rebuilding their life and moving forward with their goals. They might initially suppress their emotions to maintain their sense of control. It's important for them to allow themselves to experience and process their feelings rather than just focusing on practical matters.

Aquarius (January 20 – February 18): Aquarius often detaches during a breakup, relying on their intellectual side to move on. They might analyze the situation and focus on their independence. However, they may need to address their emotions head-on to fully heal and avoid suppressing their feelings.

Pisces (February 19 – March 20): Pisces are deeply affected by breakups and may immerse themselves in their emotions. They often need to process their feelings through creative outlets or introspection. It's crucial for them to find a balance between their emotional depth and practical steps for moving on.

Chapter 9

How to Spot a Zodiac Sign in Love

Each zodiac shows their love in different ways. Learn how to recognize when someone is falling for you based on their sign.

Here are love signals for all the zodiac signs:

Aries (March 21 - April 19): An Aries in love is bold and direct. They'll make the first move, showering you with passionate energy and grand gestures. Expect them to initiate exciting dates and take the lead in the relationship.

Taurus (April 20 - May 20): A Taurus shows love through physical touch and creating a sense of security. They'll spoil you with thoughtful gifts, home-cooked meals, and plenty of cuddles, ensuring you feel cherished and comfortable in their presence.

Gemini (May 21 - June 20): When a Gemini falls for you, they'll engage you in deep, stimulating conversations. They'll want to know every detail about you, always keeping things lively with humor, witty remarks, and spontaneous plans.

Cancer (June 21 - July 22): A Cancer in love is nurturing and protective. They'll create a warm, loving environment and offer emotional support. Expect them to prioritize your feelings, often expressing love through affectionate gestures and heartfelt words.

Leo (July 23 - August 22): A Leo in love will shower you with attention and admiration. They'll want to impress you with their creativity and generosity, often going out of their way to make you feel like the center of their universe.

Virgo (August 23 - September 22): A Virgo in love will express their affection through acts of service. From organizing your life to helping you with little tasks, their way of showing love is often practical.

Libra (September 23 - October 22): When a Libra is in love, they'll go out of their way to create harmony in the relationship. They'll be attentive to your needs, making sure you feel valued. They also enjoy romantic gestures and will put effort into planning special moments for you both.

Scorpio (October 23 - November 21): A Scorpio in love is intensely loyal and emotionally invested. They'll want to form a deep, passionate connection with you, often expressing their feelings through physical closeness and intimate conversations.

Sagittarius (November 22 - December 21): When Sagittarius falls for you, they'll want to include you in their adventures. They'll invite you on trips and try new experiences together, always keeping the relationship exciting.

Capricorn (December 22 - January 19): A Capricorn in love will show their dedication through stability and commitment. They'll take the relationship seriously, often expressing love by being reliable and working hard to build a solid future together.

Aquarius (January 20 - February 18): When an Aquarius is in love, they'll want to connect with you on an intellectual level. They'll introduce you to their unconventional interests and involve you in deep discussions about shared ideals, expressing love through friendship and unique experiences.

Pisces (February 19 - March 20): A Pisces in love will be incredibly romantic and compassionate. They'll express their affection through dreamy, emotional gestures—whether it's writing you a poem or surprising you with a thoughtful gift, they'll go above and beyond to show you how much they care.

Chapter 10

Zodiac Sexual Compatibility

Sexual compatibility is a crucial aspect of relationships, and astrology offers a deeper understanding of the desires, preferences, and natural chemistry between zodiac signs. Each zodiac sign has a distinct approach to intimacy, shaped by their element (Fire, Earth, Air, Water) and ruling planet. Understanding these tendencies can help modern daters navigate the sexual side of their relationships, ensuring that both partners' needs are met in a fulfilling and passionate way. By understanding how each zodiac sign approaches sex, daters can foster deeper connections, communicate more effectively, and ensure a more fulfilling romantic life. Whether looking for a playful Gemini or a deeply intense Scorpio, knowing the sexual tendencies of each sign can enhance both short-term connections and long-term compatibility.

In this chapter, we'll explore the sexual compatibility of the zodiac signs, revealing how each sign behaves in the bedroom, and which signs they connect with most intimately.

Fire Signs (Aries, Leo, Sagittarius): Passionate and Adventurous

> **Aries** (March 21 - April 19)
> Aries approaches sex with passion, energy, and spontaneity. They love to take the lead, initiating new experiences in the bedroom and keeping things exciting. Sexual chemistry with Aries is often immediate and fiery. They are compatible with fellow Fire signs like Leo and Sagittarius, who share their zest for life and adventure. However, Aries can clash with more reserved signs like Virgo or Cancer, who may find their intensity overwhelming.

> **Leo** (July 23 - August 22)
> Leo brings confidence and creativity to their sexual relationships. They enjoy being the center of attention, and their sexual energy is often playful and exuberant. Leos are generous lovers who seek to

impress and please their partners. They connect well with Aquarius, who challenges them intellectually and sexually, and Aries, who matches their fiery passion. Leo may struggle with more introverted signs like Capricorn, who might not give them the admiration they crave.

Sagittarius (November 22 - December 21)
Sagittarius approaches sex with a sense of freedom, fun, and exploration. They are adventurous lovers, always eager to try something new and exciting. For Sagittarius, sex is about having a good time and keeping things light. They are compatible with Gemini, who shares their playful spirit, and Aries, who can match their passion. More possessive signs like Scorpio might find Sagittarius' need for freedom challenging, leading to tension in intimate situations.

Earth Signs (Taurus, Virgo, Capricorn): Sensual and Grounded

Taurus (April 20 - May 20)
Taurus is sensual and deeply connected to physical pleasure. They prefer slow, romantic encounters and prioritize intimacy and connection. Taurus thrives in a steady, committed relationship, where trust allows them to fully enjoy the physical side of love. They are most compatible with fellow Earth signs like Virgo and Capricorn, who appreciate their sensual approach. However, they may struggle with more impulsive signs like Sagittarius, who may not align with their need for stability.

Virgo (August 23 - September 22)
Virgos are meticulous and detail-oriented, even in the bedroom. They may be reserved at first, but once they feel comfortable, they become attentive and devoted lovers, focusing on their partner's pleasure. Virgos connect well with Taurus and Capricorn, who share their practical, steady approach to intimacy. They might find more chaotic or unpredictable signs like Aries or Aquarius difficult to handle due to their need for order and structure in relationships.

Capricorn (December 22 - January 19)
Capricorn is often seen as serious and goal-oriented, but they have a deeply passionate side once they let their guard down. They prefer long-term commitments and view sex as an expression of trust and stability in a relationship. Capricorn is compatible with Virgo, who understands their need for control and practicality, and Scorpio, who appreciates their depth and intensity. Capricorns may clash with signs like Leo, who might find them too rigid or reserved.

Air Signs (Gemini, Libra, Aquarius): Intellectual and Playful

Gemini (May 21 - June 20)
Geminis are curious, playful, and unpredictable in the bedroom. They enjoy variety and intellectual stimulation, often experimenting with new ideas and approaches to intimacy. For Geminis, communication and mental connection are key to sexual attraction. They are compatible with Aquarius, who can keep up with their need for stimulation, and Sagittarius, who shares their love for spontaneity. Geminis might struggle with more emotionally intense signs like Cancer, who may seek a deeper emotional bond.

Libra (September 23 - October 22)
Libras are charming and sensual lovers, valuing beauty, harmony, and romance in their intimate relationships. They seek balance and mutual pleasure, often going to great lengths to ensure that both partners are satisfied. Libra connects well with Aries, who brings excitement and passion to their more refined approach, and Gemini, who shares their love for intellectual stimulation. Libra may struggle with signs like Capricorn, who might not prioritize the romantic and aesthetic aspects that are so important to them.

Aquarius (January 20 - February 18)
Aquarians are unconventional and open-minded when it comes to sex. They enjoy experimenting and exploring new ways of connecting with their partner. Intellectual connection is crucial for Aquarius, and they often prefer a mental bond before engaging in

physical intimacy. They are most compatible with Gemini, who stimulates them intellectually, and Libra, who shares their appreciation for balance and fairness. Aquarius may struggle with more possessive signs like Taurus, who might find their need for freedom unsettling.

Water Signs (Cancer, Scorpio, Pisces): Emotional and Intuitive

Cancer (June 21 - July 22)

Cancer approaches sex with deep emotion and vulnerability. They need to feel safe and secure in a relationship before fully opening up to intimacy. When they do, they are nurturing and affectionate lovers who seek a deep emotional connection. Cancer is most compatible with Scorpio, who understands their emotional depth, and Pisces, who shares their intuitive approach to love. However, Cancer may struggle with more detached signs like Aquarius, who might not provide the emotional warmth they need.

Scorpio (October 23 - November 21)

Scorpio is often seen as the most intense and passionate sign when it comes to sex. They crave deep, transformative experiences and are known for their magnetic sexual energy. Scorpio seeks full emotional and physical immersion in their relationships, and they are most compatible with Pisces, who matches their emotional intensity, and Capricorn, who provides the stability they crave. Scorpio may find more carefree signs like Gemini or Sagittarius difficult, as they might not meet Scorpio's emotional depth.

Pisces (February 19 - March 20)

Pisces are dreamers and romantics, approaching sex with tenderness and empathy. They seek emotional connection and often use intimacy as a way to express their love and devotion. Pisces is most compatible with Cancer, who understands their need for emotional security, and Scorpio, who provides intensity and passion. However, they may struggle with more practical signs like Virgo, who might not fully appreciate their imaginative and emotional approach to intimacy.

Chapter 11

Zodiac Love Signals by Gender

Understanding how each zodiac sign expresses love can help deepen your relationships and recognize the unique love signals of both men and women. While zodiac traits apply broadly, men and women may show love differently based on traditional gender roles and personal expression. This chapter offers insight into how men and women of each zodiac sign express their love uniquely. Understanding these signals can help you recognize when someone is showing affection and deepen your connection. Here's how each sign reveals their affection when they're in love.

Aries (March 21 - April 19)

Aries Woman: An Aries woman in love is bold and direct. She will take charge, express her feelings openly, and initiate plans for exciting dates. Her love is passionate, and she loves a challenge in a relationship.

Aries Man: An Aries man will pursue the object of his affection with intensity. He'll show his love through spontaneous actions, adventurous dates, and by constantly seeking to impress and protect his partner.

Taurus (April 20 - May 20)

Taurus Woman: Loyal and dependable, a Taurus woman shows her love through stability. She'll focus on creating a comfortable, luxurious environment for her partner, from home-cooked meals to thoughtful gifts that symbolize her commitment.

Taurus Man: A Taurus man in love is steady and affectionate. He'll demonstrate his devotion by being there when you need him, offering practical support, and showing patience as the relationship grows deeper.

Gemini (May 21 - June 20)

Gemini Woman: A Gemini woman will captivate you with her lively personality and playful communication. She'll express love by keeping the conversation exciting, sharing interesting ideas, and introducing variety in your time together.

Gemini Man: A Gemini man in love is curious and playful. He'll express affection through witty banter, frequent texts or calls, and by always keeping things interesting, making sure there's never a dull moment in the relationship.

Cancer (June 21 - July 22)

Cancer Woman: Nurturing and devoted, a Cancer woman shows her love by taking care of her partner emotionally and physically. She'll create a safe, cozy space and will be there to offer unwavering support.

Cancer Man: A Cancer man is deeply emotional and caring. He expresses love by making sure his partner feels cherished and protected, offering loyalty and comfort through small gestures of affection.

Leo (July 23 - August 22)

Leo Woman: A Leo woman in love is expressive and generous. She'll shower her partner with attention, grand romantic gestures, and make sure they feel like the center of her universe.

Leo Man: A Leo man will be bold and dramatic in his affections. He'll love to show off his partner and will express his devotion through public displays of affection, extravagant gifts, and making his partner feel special.

Virgo (August 23 - September 22)

Virgo Woman: Practical and detail-oriented, a Virgo woman shows love through acts of service. She'll help organize your life, offer advice, and quietly handle the little things to make your life easier.

Virgo Man: A Virgo man expresses love by being dependable and attentive to his partner's needs. He may not be overly emotional, but he'll show care through thoughtful actions, problem-solving, and making sure everything runs smoothly.

Libra (September 23 - October 22)

Libra Woman: A Libra woman in love is romantic and charming. She'll create a harmonious relationship, making her partner feel admired and valued through balanced, thoughtful conversations and a keen sense of partnership.

Libra Man: A Libra man expresses love by creating a peaceful and beautiful relationship. He'll seek to please his partner, paying attention to fairness and making sure the relationship feels like an equal, loving exchange.

Scorpio (October 23 - November 21)

Scorpio Woman: Passionate and intense, a Scorpio woman in love will show her feelings through loyalty and deep emotional connection. She'll express her love with powerful devotion, seeking to bond with her partner on a soul level.

Scorpio Man: A Scorpio man is protective and deeply committed. His love is expressed through loyalty, intensity, and an unwavering dedication to building a strong emotional bond with his partner.

Sagittarius (November 22 - December 21)

Sagittarius Woman: A Sagittarius woman in love is adventurous and free-spirited. She'll express affection by encouraging shared experiences and spontaneous activities, keeping the relationship fun and fresh.

Sagittarius Man: A Sagittarius man shows love by including his partner in his adventures. He'll express his affection through fun, light-hearted conversations and by making sure the relationship stays full of excitement and growth.

Capricorn (December 22 - January 19)

Capricorn Woman: Practical and ambitious, a Capricorn woman shows love through commitment and long-term planning. She'll express affection by building a stable foundation for the relationship and by supporting her partner's ambitions.

Capricorn Man: A Capricorn man is serious about love. He'll express his feelings through loyalty, consistency, and by working hard to ensure a secure future for the relationship, showing affection through his dedication.

Aquarius (January 20 - February 18)

Aquarius Woman: Independent and intellectual, an Aquarius woman will show love through deep conversations and shared ideas. She values freedom in a relationship but will express her affection by being a unique and innovative partner.

Aquarius Man: An Aquarius man in love is open-minded and unconventional. He'll express affection through intellectual connection, engaging in meaningful discussions and shared interests rather than overt romantic gestures.

Pisces (February 19 - March 20)

Pisces Woman: Romantic and empathetic, a Pisces woman shows love through emotional connection and creativity. She'll express her feelings through dreamy, artistic gestures, and by offering deep emotional understanding and care.

Pisces Man: A Pisces man is sensitive and compassionate in love. He'll express affection by being emotionally available, offering support, and creating a soulful, imaginative connection with his partner.

Chapter 12

Zodiac Compatibility Pairs by Gender

In relationships, zodiac compatibility can play an interesting role, with each sign pairing differently based on gender dynamics. While astrological traits influence the core nature of a sign, men and women may bring subtle differences in how these traits manifest in relationships. In astrology, the interplay of masculine and feminine energies can reveal unique compatibility dynamics between signs. Whether it's the nurturing Cancer woman with the intense Scorpio man, or the adventurous Sagittarius woman with the daring Aries man, understanding these zodiac-based love signals by gender offers a deeper understanding of romantic relationships.

Let's explore the most compatible pairings, considering both male and female energies in the zodiac signs. Use these insights to enhance your connection and navigate love with greater self-awareness and harmony.

Aries (March 21 - April 19)

Aries Woman & Leo Man: These two fire signs ignite passion and excitement. The Aries woman's boldness complements the Leo man's charismatic confidence. They both thrive on adventure and mutual admiration.

Aries Man & Sagittarius Woman: This adventurous duo loves exploring new horizons. The Aries man's daring nature matches the Sagittarius woman's free-spirited attitude, leading to a lively and inspiring relationship.

Taurus (April 20 - May 20)

Taurus Woman & Cancer Man: The Taurus woman craves stability, and the nurturing Cancer man offers emotional security. Together, they create a loving and supportive relationship where both feel safe and appreciated.

Taurus Man & Virgo Woman: Both practical and grounded, these earth signs build a solid foundation. The Taurus man's loyalty and the Virgo woman's attention to detail form a harmonious, long-lasting partnership.

Gemini (May 21 - June 20)

Gemini Woman & Aquarius Man: Both air signs, this pair thrives on intellectual stimulation. The Gemini woman's quick wit and the Aquarius man's progressive ideas create an exciting, mentally stimulating relationship.

Gemini Man & Libra Woman: These two love to socialize and share ideas. The Gemini man's playful charm and the Libra woman's balance and grace make them a well-matched pair in love, always keeping things fresh and fun.

Cancer (June 21 - July 22)

Cancer Woman & Scorpio Man: Emotional intensity binds this water sign couple. The Cancer woman's nurturing nature complements the Scorpio man's deep emotional intensity, creating a strong, passionate bond.

Cancer Man & Pisces Woman: This deeply emotional pairing feels like a soulmate connection. The Cancer man's protective instincts harmonize with the Pisces woman's dreamy, compassionate energy.

Leo (July 23 - August 22)

Leo Woman & Aries Man: This fiery duo has an unstoppable energy. The Leo woman's regal confidence matches well with the Aries man's bold assertiveness, creating a relationship full of passion and excitement.

Leo Man & Sagittarius Woman: Both lovers of adventure and excitement, this pairing thrives on shared experiences. The Leo man's charisma and the Sagittarius woman's love of freedom create a dynamic, spirited romance.

Virgo (August 23 - September 22)

Virgo Woman & Taurus Man: Practical and dependable, this earth sign pair works harmoniously. The Virgo woman's precision and the Taurus man's stability create a reliable and loving relationship.

Virgo Man & Capricorn Woman: Both are hardworking and goal-oriented. The Virgo man's meticulous nature blends well with the Capricorn woman's ambition, leading to a relationship built on mutual respect and shared goals.

Libra (September 23 - October 22)

Libra Woman & Gemini Man: This pairing is one of intellectual and social harmony. The Libra woman's charm and diplomacy balance well with the Gemini man's wit and curiosity, making them a socially vibrant and compatible couple.

Libra Man & Aquarius Woman: Both air signs, they value independence and intellectual connection. The Libra man's love for balance is complemented by the Aquarius woman's progressive, free-thinking nature.

Scorpio (October 23 - November 21)

Scorpio Woman & Pisces Man: Both water signs, this couple has a deep, intuitive bond. The Scorpio woman's intensity and the Pisces man's sensitivity create an emotionally rich and passionate connection.

Scorpio Man & Cancer Woman: This pairing is marked by emotional depth and loyalty. The Scorpio man's protective nature aligns perfectly with the Cancer woman's nurturing instincts, resulting in a strong and devoted relationship.

Sagittarius (November 22 - December 21)

Sagittarius Woman & Aries Man: This fiery pair thrives on excitement and adventure. The Sagittarius woman's free spirit and the Aries man's daring personality create an energetic, adventurous relationship.

Sagittarius Man & Leo Woman: Both love attention and have a zest for life. The Sagittarius man's wanderlust matches the Leo woman's passion for the spotlight, creating a relationship full of fun and enthusiasm.

Capricorn (December 22 - January 19)

Capricorn Woman & Virgo Man: Both earth signs, this pair shares a practical and determined approach to life. The Capricorn woman's ambition complements the Virgo man's attention to detail, creating a relationship built on mutual goals.

Capricorn Man & Taurus Woman: This duo appreciates stability and loyalty. The Capricorn man's dedication and the Taurus woman's steadfast nature create a strong, enduring bond based on shared values.

Aquarius (January 20 - February 18)

Aquarius Woman & Libra Man: Both intellectual air signs, they form a mentally stimulating connection. The Aquarius woman's individuality and the Libra man's charm create a balanced and intellectually rich relationship.

Aquarius Man & Gemini Woman: This pair thrives on communication and intellectual curiosity. The Aquarius man's innovative mind and the Gemini woman's versatility create a relationship full of stimulating conversation and shared ideas.

Pisces (February 19 - March 20)

Pisces Woman & Scorpio Man: This intense water sign pairing creates a deep, emotional connection. The Pisces woman's sensitivity aligns well with the Scorpio man's passion, forming a bond that feels spiritual and transformative.

Pisces Man & Cancer Woman: Emotional and intuitive, this pairing forms a nurturing and caring relationship. The Pisces man's compassionate nature blends beautifully with the Cancer woman's warmth and care, creating a harmonious and emotionally fulfilling love.

Chapter 13

The Sexual Traits of Each Zodiac Woman

In astrology, every zodiac sign carries unique energy, influencing how individuals express themselves, especially in intimate relationships. For women, sexual traits can vary dramatically depending on their zodiac sign, revealing different desires, tendencies, and approaches to romance and pleasure. Let's dive into the sexual traits of women from each zodiac sign.

Aries Woman (March 21 - April 19)

The Aries woman is fiery, confident, and passionate. She approaches sex with a sense of adventure and excitement, often taking the lead in the bedroom. Bold and direct, she enjoys spontaneity and isn't afraid to express her desires openly. Her strong will and independence can make her an energetic lover who craves intensity and thrill. However, she expects her partner to match her energy and enthusiasm, often getting bored with routine. An Aries woman values both passion and conquest, thriving on the chase and the chemistry that comes with it.

Taurus Woman (April 20 - May 20)

Ruled by Venus, the planet of love and beauty, the Taurus woman is sensual and deeply connected to physical pleasure. She loves to indulge in all things that stimulate the senses—touch, taste, smell, and sound. A Taurus woman desires a slow, patient lover who takes time to appreciate every moment. She finds great satisfaction in the buildup to intimacy and prefers deep, romantic connections that lead to passionate lovemaking. While she may take time to open up, once she does, her sexual energy is grounded, steady, and deeply fulfilling.

Gemini Woman (May 21 - June 20)

Curious, playful, and flirtatious, the Gemini woman brings intellectual stimulation into the bedroom. She thrives on variety and mental connection, often incorporating humor and witty banter into her seduction style. Her sexual energy is light-hearted and fun, and she's open to experimenting with new ideas, locations, and techniques. However, a Gemini woman can sometimes be unpredictable or inconsistent in her desires, and her mind may wander if she gets bored. She craves a lover who can keep up with her quick wit and adapt to her ever-changing mood.

Cancer Woman (June 21 - July 22)

The Cancer woman is deeply emotional and intuitive, bringing a nurturing and protective energy to her sexual relationships. She needs to feel emotionally secure and loved before fully opening up in the bedroom. Once she feels safe, her sexual expression is tender, affectionate, and highly sensual. She connects on an emotional and spiritual level with her partner, prioritizing intimacy over casual encounters. Her love language is about creating a warm, safe space, where both partners can explore their deepest desires and vulnerabilities.

Leo Woman (July 23 - August 22)

Bold, passionate, and self-assured, the Leo woman craves attention and adoration in the bedroom. She loves to be worshipped and isn't shy about letting her partner know what she wants. A true queen of seduction, she enjoys a playful, extravagant approach to sex, where she can express her dramatic side. The Leo woman desires to feel special and cherished, often seeking grand romantic gestures that make her feel like the center of her partner's world. She brings intensity, excitement, and a generous heart to her sexual relationships.

Virgo Woman (August 23 - September 22)

The Virgo woman is often perceived as reserved or modest, but beneath that exterior lies a passionate and attentive lover. Known for her perfectionism, she is detail-oriented in bed, often taking the time to learn what pleases her partner. A Virgo woman is practical but deeply sensual, craving a strong intellectual connection that can evolve into physical intimacy. She appreciates cleanliness, comfort, and a partner who is as thoughtful and caring as she is. When trust is established, her passionate nature unfolds in a precise and deeply satisfying way.

Libra Woman (September 23 - October 22)

Ruled by Venus, the Libra woman is all about balance, beauty, and harmony in her sexual relationships. She is romantic, charming, and seeks a partner who appreciates elegance and refinement in the bedroom. For the Libra woman, sex is an art form—she loves creating a beautiful and harmonious environment for intimacy. She craves a deep emotional connection, often prioritizing the emotional and mental aspects of love over purely physical ones. A natural giver, she seeks fairness in bed, always aiming to ensure mutual pleasure and satisfaction.

Scorpio Woman (October 23 - November 21)

The Scorpio woman is known for her intense, magnetic sexual energy. She is mysterious, passionate, and craves deep emotional and physical intimacy. With her, sex is a transformative experience, often involving intense emotions and powerful desires. The Scorpio woman doesn't shy away from exploring taboo or hidden aspects of sexuality and expects total vulnerability from her partner. She has an almost magnetic allure, drawing others in with her mysterious and seductive nature. For a Scorpio woman, sex is an all-or-nothing experience, and she seeks a partner who can match her intensity.

Sagittarius Woman (November 22 - December 21)

Fun-loving, adventurous, and free-spirited, the Sagittarius woman approaches sex with a sense of exploration and excitement. She is open-minded, always eager to try new things, and enjoys a carefree, spontaneous approach to intimacy. For her, sex is an adventure, and she often seeks partners who share her enthusiasm for new experiences. A Sagittarius woman values her freedom and may shy away from overly emotional or possessive partners. Her sexual relationships are often light-hearted and full of laughter, but she's always seeking a deeper truth and understanding through her intimate encounters.

Capricorn Woman (December 22 - January 19)

Ambitious and disciplined, the Capricorn woman approaches sex with the same focus and determination she applies to all areas of her life. She may come across as reserved, but underneath, she is deeply passionate and sensual. A Capricorn woman is a slow burner, preferring a stable, reliable partner with whom she can build a long-term, satisfying sexual connection. She values consistency and loyalty in her relationships, and once trust is earned, she can be an incredibly giving and devoted lover. While she may not be spontaneous, her commitment and depth of passion make her a powerful force in the bedroom.

Aquarius Woman (January 20 - February 18)

The Aquarius woman is unconventional, open-minded, and always looking to push the boundaries of traditional intimacy. She craves intellectual stimulation in her sexual relationships and is attracted to partners who challenge her mind. The Aquarius woman is often experimental and may be interested in exploring non-traditional forms of sexuality. While she values independence and freedom, she is deeply committed to her principles and can form strong, lasting bonds with partners who respect her need for personal space. Her sexual energy is innovative and electric, making her a fascinating and unpredictable lover.

Pisces Woman (February 19 - March 20)

Dreamy, sensitive, and intuitive, the Pisces woman brings a deep emotional connection to her sexual relationships. She is often highly attuned to her partner's needs and desires, creating an almost spiritual experience in the bedroom. For her, sex is a way to connect on a soul level, blending emotional, physical, and spiritual energies. A Pisces woman is compassionate and giving, often losing herself in her partner's pleasure. She seeks a partner who can reciprocate her deep emotional intensity and help her explore the depths of love and intimacy.

Chapter 14

The Sexual Traits of Each Zodiac Man

Just as the stars influence women's romantic and sexual traits, they also play a significant role in shaping how men approach intimacy, passion, and connection. Each zodiac sign brings unique strengths, tendencies, and desires into the bedroom. Understanding these traits can provide valuable insights into your partner's sexual style and preferences.

Aries Man (March 21 - April 19)

The Aries man is bold, assertive, and often takes the lead in the bedroom. He is passionate, spontaneous, and enjoys the thrill of the chase. An Aries man approaches sex with high energy and excitement, seeking adventure and variety in his encounters. He tends to be direct and doesn't shy away from expressing his desires. For him, physical attraction and conquest are key, and he thrives on the chemistry of a new partner. However, his impatience can sometimes lead to a focus on instant gratification, and he may lose interest if the relationship lacks excitement.

Taurus Man (April 20 - May 20)

The Taurus man is sensual, patient, and highly attuned to physical pleasure. Ruled by Venus, the planet of love, he takes his time in the bedroom, savoring every moment. A Taurus man craves comfort and luxury, often preferring a romantic and indulgent approach to intimacy. He enjoys touch and affection, making him a highly attentive lover. Once committed, he is loyal and steadfast, seeking long-term, stable relationships. While he may not be the most adventurous, his steady and reliable nature ensures that his partner feels cherished and satisfied.

Gemini Man (May 21 - June 20)

The Gemini man is playful, curious, and often approaches sex with a light-hearted attitude. He is intellectually driven and needs mental stimulation to maintain interest in a relationship. A Gemini man enjoys variety and can be quite flirtatious, often exploring new ideas and techniques in the bedroom. His sexual energy is youthful and fun, and he's likely to keep things exciting with spontaneity and humor. However, his restlessness and desire for novelty can make him inconsistent, and he may struggle with commitment if the relationship becomes too routine.

Cancer Man (June 21 - July 22)

Deeply emotional and nurturing, the Cancer man is a sensitive and affectionate lover. He seeks security and emotional connection in his sexual relationships, often approaching intimacy with a protective and caring demeanor. A Cancer man is highly intuitive and attuned to his partner's needs, making him a compassionate and giving lover. He prefers long-term relationships where he can form deep emotional bonds and feels most fulfilled when he can nurture and support his partner. However, his sensitivity can make him vulnerable to emotional wounds, and he needs a partner who provides reassurance and emotional stability.

Leo Man (July 23 - August 22)

The Leo man is confident, charismatic, and enjoys being the center of attention, both in life and in the bedroom. He approaches sex with a sense of playfulness and drama, often seeking to impress his partner with grand gestures and passionate displays of affection. A Leo man loves to be admired and praised, and he thrives in relationships where he feels appreciated and adored. He is generous in the bedroom and enjoys making his partner feel special. However, his need for validation can sometimes lead to ego-driven behavior, and he may become frustrated if he feels his efforts go unnoticed.

Virgo Man (August 23 - September 22)

The Virgo man is meticulous, attentive, and highly analytical, even when it comes to sex. He takes his time to understand his partner's needs and desires, often approaching intimacy with care and precision. A Virgo man may seem reserved or modest at first, but once he feels comfortable, he becomes a dedicated and thoughtful lover. He values cleanliness, order, and routine, and his sexual style reflects his practical nature. While he may not be the most spontaneous, his attention to detail ensures that his partner feels well taken care of and deeply satisfied.

Libra Man (September 23 - October 22)

Ruled by Venus, the planet of love and beauty, the Libra man is a romantic and charming lover. He seeks balance and harmony in his sexual relationships, always striving to create a beautiful and pleasurable experience for his partner. A Libra man is generous and fair in bed, ensuring that both partners are equally satisfied. He is highly attuned to the aesthetics of romance, enjoying candlelit dinners, soft music, and other romantic gestures that set the mood. However, his desire to avoid conflict can sometimes lead to indecisiveness or a lack of assertiveness.

Scorpio Man (October 23 - November 21)

The Scorpio man is known for his intense, magnetic sexual energy. He is passionate, deeply emotional, and seeks transformative experiences in the bedroom. For a Scorpio man, sex is not just a physical act but a way to connect on a deep, soulful level. He craves total emotional and physical intimacy, often pushing boundaries to explore the depths of desire. His allure is powerful, and he can be both mysterious and seductive. However, his intensity can also lead to possessiveness or jealousy, and he needs a partner who can handle his emotional depth and desire for control.

Sagittarius Man (November 22 - December 21)

Fun-loving, adventurous, and free-spirited, the Sagittarius man approaches sex with a sense of exploration and excitement. He is open-minded and enjoys trying new things, often seeking out partners who share his love for adventure. A Sagittarius man is playful in the bedroom and enjoys keeping things light and fun. He values his freedom and may shy away from overly emotional or possessive partners. While he enjoys casual flings and spontaneous encounters, he is also capable of forming deep connections with partners who share his zest for life and intellectual curiosity.

Capricorn Man (December 22 - January 19)

Ambitious, disciplined, and often reserved, the Capricorn man approaches sex with a sense of responsibility and commitment. He may take time to open up emotionally, but once he does, he is a passionate and dedicated lover. A Capricorn man values stability and long-term relationships, often seeking partners who share his goals and ambitions. In the bedroom, he is patient, reliable, and focused on providing satisfaction for his partner. While he may not be the most spontaneous, his steady nature and deep sense of loyalty make him a dependable and thoughtful lover.

Aquarius Man (January 20 - February 18)

The Aquarius man is unconventional, intellectual, and always looking to push boundaries in his sexual relationships. He is attracted to partners who stimulate his mind and share his progressive views on love and intimacy. A true nonconformist, the Aquarius man may explore non-traditional relationships or sexual experiences, often valuing emotional independence and freedom. While he may seem detached at times, he is deeply committed to his ideals and can form strong, lasting bonds with partners who respect his need for space. His sexual energy is inventive and unique, making him an exciting and unpredictable lover.

Pisces Man (February 19 - March 20)

The Pisces man is dreamy, sensitive, and deeply romantic. He seeks emotional and spiritual connection in his sexual relationships, often approaching intimacy with a compassionate and selfless attitude. A Pisces man is attuned to his partner's emotional needs and desires, often going out of his way to create a magical, otherworldly experience in the bedroom. He is a giver in love, prioritizing his partner's pleasure and happiness above his own. His sexual energy is intuitive and emotionally charged, making him a deeply empathetic and caring lover.

Understanding the sexual traits of each zodiac man can help you navigate the complexities of intimacy and relationships. Whether you're looking for passion, stability, or adventure, astrology provides insights into how your partner expresses love and desire, helping you deepen your connection and enrich your romantic experiences.

Chapter 15

Zodiac Love Cycles: How Each Sign Navigates the Phases of Relationships

Each zodiac sign approaches relationships with its own rhythm, moving through the stages of love in unique ways. Whether they fall fast and hard or take their time to commit, the stars influence how individuals experience the ebb and flow of romance—from dating, to deep passion, to long-term stability. In this chapter, we'll explore how each zodiac sign navigates these love cycles, and how their sexual behavior evolves as they progress through the stages of a relationship.

Aries (March 21 - April 19): The Passionate Trailblazer

Aries are known for their fiery, go-getter approach to relationships. In the early stages of dating, they are bold, direct, and love the thrill of the chase. Aries fall quickly and passionately, and their sexual energy reflects this intensity. They are spontaneous lovers who enjoy excitement and adventure in the bedroom.

As the relationship moves forward, Aries may struggle with the monotony of stability. However, if their partner can keep things fresh and stimulating, Aries can stay engaged. Their sexual passion remains high, but they need constant action and novelty to keep the fire alive.

Taurus (April 20 - May 20): The Slow-Burning Lover

Taurus takes their time in relationships, preferring to build a strong foundation of trust before diving into deeper intimacy. In the dating phase, they may seem cautious, but once they feel secure, their sensual side shines through. Taurus values touch and physical connection, and their sexual style is deliberate and deeply intimate.

As the relationship matures, Taurus craves stability and comfort. They are loyal and reliable partners who enjoy routine and consistency. In the bedroom, they continue to be attentive lovers, though they may prefer a slower, more romantic pace rather than wild experimentation.

Gemini (May 21 - June 20): The Playful Communicator

Gemini's love life is marked by curiosity and intellectual stimulation. During the dating phase, they are flirty, witty, and love to keep things light. Gemini thrives on mental connection, and their sexual behavior can be unpredictable, shifting between fun and intense as they explore different facets of their attraction.

As the relationship evolves, Gemini may struggle with commitment, needing variety to stay interested. However, if their partner can keep them mentally engaged, Gemini can settle into a stable relationship without losing their playful, experimental edge in the bedroom.

Cancer (June 21 - July 22): The Emotional Nurturer

Cancer approaches relationships with deep emotional vulnerability. They fall in love cautiously, needing to feel secure before opening up completely. In the early stages, they may appear reserved, but once trust is built, they reveal a deeply passionate and caring lover. Cancer's sexual behavior is tied closely to their emotions, so when they feel loved, they are attentive and giving.

As the relationship matures, Cancer desires long-term commitment and emotional security. They crave emotional and physical intimacy, and their sexual energy remains nurturing and focused on creating a deep bond with their partner.

Leo (July 23 - August 22): The Passionate Performer

Leo thrives on romance, excitement, and adoration. In the early stages of dating, they are charming and magnetic, drawing their partner in with confidence and flair. Leo's sexual energy is passionate and creative, as they enjoy being the center of attention and seek to impress in all areas of the relationship.

As the relationship deepens, Leo remains devoted and loyal, though they need constant affection and praise to feel valued. In a stable relationship,

Leo's sexual behavior remains fiery and expressive, with a focus on keeping the passion alive.

Virgo (August 23 - September 22): The Thoughtful Partner

Virgo approaches love with caution and practicality. During the dating phase, they may appear reserved, preferring to get to know their partner slowly. Virgo's sexual behavior reflects their thoughtful nature—they are attentive lovers who seek to please but may be slow to fully express their desires.

As the relationship evolves, Virgo focuses on building a stable, reliable partnership. They are highly committed and dedicated to their partner's well-being. In the bedroom, Virgo's sexual behavior becomes more open as they feel more secure, often taking a nurturing and detail-oriented approach to intimacy.

Libra (September 23 - October 22): The Romantic Idealist

Libra loves love and seeks harmony in relationships. During the dating phase, they are charming, flirtatious, and often fall for the idea of romance. Libra's sexual behavior is sensual and balanced—they enjoy creating a beautiful and romantic atmosphere and prioritize their partner's pleasure.

As the relationship moves toward stability, Libra may struggle with indecision but ultimately seeks balance and partnership. In a long-term relationship, Libra continues to value sexual and emotional connection, keeping the romance alive through constant attention to their partner's needs.

Scorpio (October 23 - November 21): The Intense Lover

Scorpio experiences love with deep intensity from the very beginning. In the dating phase, they are mysterious and magnetic, drawing their partner in with passion and intrigue. Scorpio's sexual behavior is all-consuming—they seek emotional and physical depth and often connect through intense intimacy.

As the relationship progresses, Scorpio demands loyalty and honesty. They may struggle with trust but, once secure, are deeply committed partners. In a stable relationship, their sexual intensity remains, and they seek to constantly explore new depths of intimacy with their partner.

Sagittarius (November 22 - December 21): The Adventurous Spirit

Sagittarius approaches relationships with a carefree, adventurous attitude. In the dating phase, they are fun-loving and spontaneous, often avoiding emotional attachment in favor of enjoying the moment. Sagittarius' sexual behavior is playful and adventurous, preferring lighthearted and explorative encounters.

As the relationship progresses, Sagittarius may resist commitment, needing freedom to stay engaged. However, in the right partnership, they can balance their love for adventure with deeper emotional connection, bringing excitement and passion to the bedroom even in long-term relationships.

Capricorn (December 22 - January 19): The Committed Builder

Capricorn takes a traditional and goal-oriented approach to relationships. During the dating phase, they may seem reserved, focusing on building a solid foundation before diving into passion. Capricorn's sexual behavior is deliberate and controlled, but as they grow comfortable, they reveal a deeply sensual side.

As the relationship matures, Capricorn values stability and long-term commitment. They are reliable, loyal partners who take their responsibilities seriously. In the bedroom, Capricorn's passion deepens over time, and they become increasingly devoted to satisfying their partner.

Aquarius (January 20 - February 18): The Unconventional Lover

Aquarius brings a unique, unconventional approach to relationships. In the dating phase, they are intellectual and curious, often preferring mental stimulation over physical intimacy. Aquarius' sexual behavior is unpredictable and experimental, reflecting their open-mindedness and desire for novelty.

As the relationship evolves, Aquarius seeks a partnership built on mutual respect and shared ideals. Though they may resist traditional relationship structures, Aquarius can be deeply loyal. Their sexual behavior continues to be experimental, valuing emotional and intellectual connection as much as physical intimacy.

Pisces (February 19 - March 20): The Dreamy Romantic

Pisces approaches love with a dreamy, idealistic view. During the dating phase, they are deeply romantic, often getting lost in their emotions and fantasies. Pisces' sexual behavior is highly intuitive and emotionally driven—they seek to merge with their partner on a spiritual and emotional level.

As the relationship deepens, Pisces remains deeply devoted and affectionate. They value emotional and sexual connection, often using intimacy as a way to express their boundless love and devotion. In a stable relationship, Pisces continues to bring creativity and emotional depth to the bedroom.

Conclusion

Each zodiac sign brings a unique rhythm to the phases of love, from the early excitement of dating to the stability of long-term commitment. Understanding how your sign—and your partner's sign—navigates these cycles can deepen your connection and create a more fulfilling romantic and sexual experience. Whether you're in the early stages of love or have been together for years, astrology provides a map to understanding the complex and evolving nature of relationships.

Chapter 16

The Emotional Needs of Each Zodiac in Relationship

Understanding the emotional needs of your partner is key to cultivating a loving and fulfilling relationship. Each zodiac sign has unique emotional desires that influence how they connect with others, what they need to feel secure, and how they express love. In this chapter, we'll dive deep into the emotional side of love and sex, revealing what each zodiac sign requires to feel truly fulfilled in a relationship.

Aries (March 21 - April 19): The Independent Adventurer

Aries thrives on excitement, passion, and independence in a relationship. Emotionally, they need a partner who respects their need for freedom while fueling their drive for adventure. They crave spontaneity and challenges, both in and out of the bedroom, and often express love through bold actions rather than words. Aries needs a partner who keeps up with their energy, gives them space to lead, and supports their ambitions.

To feel emotionally secure, Aries also requires respect and recognition for their efforts. They need a relationship that's constantly evolving and pushing boundaries, preventing any feelings of stagnation.

Taurus (April 20 - May 20): The Sensual Provider

Taurus craves stability and comfort in relationships, and their emotional needs reflect a desire for loyalty, trust, and consistency. They thrive in environments where they feel safe and secure, and they need a partner who can provide a sense of calm. For Taurus, emotional security often comes from building a reliable, grounded partnership.

Physically affectionate and deeply sensual, Taurus expresses love through touch and shared experiences. They need to feel appreciated, valued, and emotionally secure in order to open up and fully trust their partner. Routine and consistency are their emotional anchors.

Gemini (May 21 - June 20): The Curious Communicator

Gemini's emotional needs are deeply tied to intellectual connection and communication. They thrive on engaging conversations, mental stimulation, and variety. To feel emotionally fulfilled, Gemini requires a partner who can keep up with their quick mind and provide constant dialogue and interaction.

In relationships, Gemini seeks someone who can adapt to their ever-changing moods and ideas. Emotional security for Gemini comes through open communication, fun, and a balance of freedom and companionship. Without mental stimulation, they may become restless or distant.

Cancer (June 21 - July 22): The Nurturing Protector

Cancer is highly emotional, sensitive, and intuitive. To feel secure in a relationship, they need a deep emotional bond with their partner. Cancer thrives on feeling needed, and they naturally assume the role of caregiver. They require constant emotional reassurance and affection to feel valued and loved.

Emotional security for Cancer comes from consistency, loyalty, and a sense of home with their partner. They are deeply empathetic and expect their partner to be equally attuned to their feelings. Cancer needs to feel emotionally safe before they can open up sexually or emotionally.

Leo (July 23 - August 22): The Confident Lover

Leo craves affection, admiration, and attention in relationships. To feel emotionally fulfilled, they need to be the center of their partner's world, receiving constant compliments, praise, and displays of love. Leo is generous and warm-hearted but also needs emotional validation to feel secure in their relationship.

For Leo, love is a grand gesture, and they need to feel adored and respected in return. Emotional security comes from knowing that their partner recognizes their value and appreciates their loyalty. Without affection and attention, Leo may feel emotionally neglected.

Virgo (August 23 - September 22): The Devoted Analyst

Virgo's emotional needs are centered around stability, trust, and practical support. While they may not be the most overtly emotional sign, they express love through acts of service and attention to detail. Virgo thrives on feeling useful and appreciated, and they need a partner who values their thoughtful nature.

To feel emotionally secure, Virgo requires a reliable and consistent partner who offers them mental and emotional stability. They need someone who understands their desire for perfection and doesn't push them too far outside of their comfort zone. Emotional fulfillment for Virgo comes from shared goals and quiet, steady support.

Libra (September 23 - October 22): The Harmonious Idealist

Libra craves balance, harmony, and connection in relationships. Emotionally, they need peace and partnership, thriving in environments that avoid conflict and drama. Libra values fairness and equality, and they need a partner who can maintain emotional equilibrium and engage in open, honest communication.

To feel secure, Libra requires a strong emotional bond based on shared ideals and mutual respect. They are romantics at heart and feel emotionally fulfilled when they are able to create beauty and harmony in their relationship, both emotionally and physically.

Scorpio (October 23 - November 21): The Intense Transformer

Scorpio is a deeply emotional and passionate sign, craving intensity and depth in relationships. Emotional security for Scorpio comes from trust, loyalty, and the ability to form a deep, transformative connection with their partner. They are naturally guarded and need to feel completely safe before revealing their vulnerability.

Scorpio's emotional needs revolve around loyalty and honesty—they demand a partner who is fully committed. When they feel emotionally secure, Scorpio is an incredibly loyal and devoted partner, offering profound intimacy and a deep emotional bond.

Sagittarius (November 22 - December 21): The Free-Spirited Explorer

Sagittarius needs freedom and adventure in their relationships to feel emotionally fulfilled. They crave novelty, excitement, and intellectual stimulation, often avoiding emotional heaviness or routine. Sagittarius values a partner who respects their need for independence and doesn't try to confine them with emotional demands.

Emotional security for Sagittarius comes from having the space to explore and grow within the relationship. They thrive when they feel free to be themselves, and a partner who can match their adventurous spirit and curiosity will keep them emotionally engaged.

Capricorn (December 22 - January 19): The Steadfast Builder

Capricorn's emotional needs revolve around stability, respect, and long-term commitment. They approach relationships with caution, building emotional connections slowly but surely. For Capricorn, emotional security comes from knowing that their partner is reliable, dedicated, and shares their long-term vision for the relationship.

Capricorn expresses love through loyalty, hard work, and practical support. They need a partner who appreciates their efforts and understands their need for structure. Once they feel emotionally secure, Capricorn is a deeply committed and protective partner.

Aquarius (January 20 - February 18): The Unconventional Idealist

Aquarius values intellectual stimulation and freedom in relationships. Emotionally, they need a partner who understands and respects their need for independence and doesn't confine them with emotional expectations. Aquarius thrives in partnerships that allow for personal growth and exploration of new ideas.

Emotional security for Aquarius comes from a deep intellectual connection, shared values, and the freedom to pursue their interests. They need a partner who supports their individuality and offers them the space to be unconventional without judgment.

Pisces (February 19 - March 20): The Empathetic Dreamer

Pisces is highly emotional, intuitive, and deeply empathetic. To feel emotionally secure in a relationship, they need a partner who can offer them emotional support, compassion, and understanding. Pisces thrives on feeling connected to their partner's emotions, often absorbing their feelings.

Pisces craves deep emotional intimacy and a spiritual connection with their partner. They are generous lovers who express love through acts of kindness and self-sacrifice. Emotional security for Pisces comes from a partner who can match their emotional depth and offer them unconditional love.

Conclusion

Every zodiac sign has unique emotional needs in relationships, shaped by their innate characteristics and desires. By understanding the emotional side of your zodiac sign—and that of your partner—you can create a more harmonious, supportive, and fulfilling relationship. Whether you're nurturing a new romance or deepening a long-term connection, meeting these emotional needs can pave the way for a more secure and emotionally rewarding partnership.

Chapter 17

Astrology and Sexual Healing: Using Your Sign to Rebuild Intimacy

Sexual healing is an essential part of emotional and physical recovery after a breakup, betrayal, or trauma. When trust is shattered or self-confidence is shaken, rebuilding intimacy can feel like an overwhelming challenge. Astrology offers a unique lens through which we can understand our sexual and emotional needs, providing guidance to help us heal and reframe our experiences. Each zodiac sign has its own path to recovery, using its strengths to regain confidence, restore trust, and foster healthier, more fulfilling relationships.

In this chapter, we explore how each zodiac sign can use their innate qualities to heal from past wounds and rebuild intimate connections with themselves and others.

Aries (March 21 - April 19): Reclaiming Power Through Passion

For Aries, healing comes through action and reclaiming their inner power. As a fire sign, Aries thrives on passion and intensity, and after emotional or sexual trauma, they must channel their energy into something positive and invigorating. Physical activity, whether through sports, dance, or intense exercise, can help Aries release pent-up emotions and boost their confidence.

In relationships, Aries heals by taking charge and setting new boundaries. It's essential for them to assert their needs, relearn trust on their terms, and regain control over their sexual experiences. Aries should focus on rekindling their passion, but with mindfulness and a clear understanding of their emotional desires.

Taurus (April 20 - May 20): Healing Through Sensuality and Stability

Taurus craves stability, comfort, and sensuality. To heal from sexual wounds, Taurus must first focus on creating a safe, nurturing environment for themselves. Grounding activities, such as cooking, gardening, or spending time in nature, can help Taurus reconnect with their body and feel secure in their own skin again.

When it comes to rebuilding intimacy, Taurus benefits from taking things slow. They need time to trust their partner fully and should prioritize sensual, physical touch that feels safe and reassuring. Taurus heals through consistency and slow, intentional steps toward regaining confidence in their body and their emotional connections.

Gemini (May 21 - June 20): Healing Through Communication and Exploration

Gemini's healing process is deeply rooted in communication and intellectual stimulation. After a breakup or emotional trauma, Gemini must express their thoughts and feelings, whether through journaling, therapy, or talking with trusted friends. Verbalizing their emotions is key to understanding and processing their pain.

Sexually, Gemini heals by exploring new ideas and rediscovering their playful nature. Trying new things in the bedroom or exploring different forms of intimacy with a partner helps them feel more in control. For Gemini, healing comes from mental stimulation and the freedom to approach intimacy in a light, fun way, without pressure or judgment.

Cancer (June 21 - July 22): Healing Through Emotional Connection

As one of the most emotionally sensitive signs, Cancer requires deep emotional healing before they can fully engage in sexual intimacy again. After trauma or heartbreak, Cancer must create a safe space where they can process their emotions, often through crying, self-care rituals, or talking with loved ones. Cancer benefits from nurturing activities like cooking, spending time with family, or taking care of pets to soothe their heart.

In relationships, Cancer heals by slowly rebuilding trust. They need a partner who can provide emotional reassurance and patience as they work through their pain. Once Cancer feels emotionally secure, they can begin to heal sexually, focusing on intimacy that feels nurturing, gentle, and deeply connected.

Leo (July 23 - August 22): Rebuilding Confidence Through Self-Love

Leo thrives on attention, validation, and self-expression. When their confidence is shattered after a breakup or sexual trauma, Leo must reconnect with their inner strength and sense of self-worth. Healing for Leo begins with practicing self-love and reclaiming their self-confidence through activities that make them feel seen and appreciated. Whether it's through creative expression, socializing with friends, or engaging in hobbies that showcase their talents, Leo heals by shining in their own light again.

Sexually, Leo heals by surrounding themselves with positivity and partners who make them feel adored and valued. They need to feel like the center of their partner's attention, receiving praise and affection to help rebuild their confidence in intimacy.

Virgo (August 23 - September 22): Healing Through Self-Care and Structure

Virgo is a sign that thrives on order, routine, and self-care. After emotional or sexual trauma, Virgo needs to regain a sense of control and organization in their life. Healing begins by focusing on their health, both mental and physical. Virgo can benefit from creating new routines that prioritize their well-being, such as meditation, exercise, or spending time in nature.

In relationships, Virgo heals by setting clear boundaries and taking a practical approach to rebuilding trust. They may feel more comfortable taking small, calculated steps toward intimacy, ensuring that they feel emotionally and physically safe at each stage. Virgo heals by creating a structured path to emotional and sexual recovery.

Libra (September 23 - October 22): Healing Through Balance and Harmony

Libra seeks balance, harmony, and peace in relationships. After experiencing heartbreak or sexual trauma, Libra must focus on restoring emotional equilibrium in their life. Surrounding themselves with beauty, whether through art, music, or nature, can help Libra feel more centered and calmer. Engaging in creative outlets can also be a powerful form of emotional healing for Libra.

In terms of intimacy, Libra heals by finding a partner who offers emotional balance and open communication. They need a relationship that feels fair and harmonious, with plenty of give-and-take. Libra thrives in relationships where they feel emotionally secure and supported in their healing journey.

Scorpio (October 23 - November 21): Healing Through Transformation and Depth

Scorpio is one of the most intense and emotionally driven signs, especially when it comes to sexual intimacy. After a breakup or emotional trauma, Scorpio must undergo a period of deep self-reflection and transformation. For Scorpio, healing often requires confronting their pain head-on, diving deep into their emotions, and emerging stronger on the other side. Therapy, shadow work, or journaling can be particularly effective for Scorpio's emotional recovery.

Sexually, Scorpio heals by reclaiming their power. They need a partner who can match their emotional depth and intensity, offering loyalty and trust. Once Scorpio feels emotionally healed, they are capable of experiencing deep, transformative sexual connections.

Sagittarius (November 22 - December 21): Healing Through Freedom and Adventure

Sagittarius is a free-spirited sign that craves adventure and exploration. After a breakup or trauma, Sagittarius heals by rediscovering their sense of freedom. Traveling, learning new things, and engaging in outdoor activities can help Sagittarius reconnect with their adventurous side and regain their zest for life.

In relationships, Sagittarius heals by taking things lightly and avoiding emotional heaviness. They need a partner who offers them space to explore and grow, both emotionally and sexually. Sagittarius heals through new experiences and keeping the energy in their relationships light, fun, and carefree.

Capricorn (December 22 - January 19): Healing Through Patience and Self-Discipline

Capricorn is a sign that values stability, discipline, and long-term commitment. When dealing with emotional or sexual trauma, Capricorn heals by setting long-term goals for their recovery. They need to feel in control of the healing process, using their patience and practicality to slowly rebuild their emotional and physical well-being.

Sexually, Capricorn heals by taking things slow. They require a partner who respects their boundaries and offers a stable, grounded environment for intimacy. Capricorn thrives in relationships that provide emotional security and a clear path toward long-term connection.

Aquarius (January 20 - February 18): Healing Through Detachment and Innovation

Aquarius is an intellectual and unconventional sign that heals by detaching from their emotions and approaching them from a logical perspective. After a breakup or trauma, Aquarius needs to take a step back and analyze their feelings before moving forward. Engaging in innovative projects, social causes, or intellectual pursuits helps Aquarius shift their focus and heal emotionally.

In relationships, Aquarius heals by finding a partner who respects their need for independence and intellectual connection. Sexual healing for Aquarius comes through experimentation and exploring new, unconventional forms of intimacy without emotional pressure.

Pisces (February 19 - March 20): Healing Through Emotional Release and Compassion

Pisces is an emotionally sensitive sign that absorbs the energy of those around them. After emotional or sexual trauma, Pisces must focus on releasing their emotions and practicing self-compassion. Engaging in creative outlets like art, music, or poetry can help Pisces express their feelings and begin the healing process.

In relationships, Pisces heals by creating deep emotional connections with a partner who offers empathy and understanding. Pisces needs a safe, nurturing space to express their emotions freely before they can rebuild sexual intimacy. Once they feel emotionally supported, Pisces can experience profound emotional and sexual healing.

Conclusion

Healing from sexual and emotional trauma is a deeply personal journey, and each zodiac sign has its unique strengths and challenges in the process. By understanding how astrology can guide your path to recovery, you can reclaim your sense of self, rebuild intimacy, and foster healthier, more fulfilling romantic relationships. Whether through passion, communication, emotional depth, or self-love, astrology offers a powerful framework for healing and renewal.

Chapter 18

Dating Red Flags for Every Zodiac Sign

When it comes to love and relationships, each zodiac sign has its strengths and weaknesses. While astrology can offer incredible insights into compatibility, it can also help us recognize potential warning signs and red flags in partners. This chapter explores the red flags for each zodiac sign, allowing you to approach relationships with clarity and awareness. By knowing what to watch out for, you can protect yourself from unnecessary heartbreak and navigate love with confidence.

Aries (March 21 - April 19): Impulsiveness and Aggression

Aries is ruled by Mars, the planet of passion and war, which means they can be fiery, direct, and often impulsive. While their energy can be exciting, one major red flag is their tendency to rush into relationships without thinking things through. If an Aries partner seems overly pushy or impatient, especially when it comes to commitment or physical intimacy, it's important to set boundaries. Aries can also have a short temper, so if their aggression flares up during conflicts, take it as a sign that they may struggle with handling emotional confrontations maturely.

Red Flag Warning: If your Aries partner is constantly pressuring you to move faster in the relationship than you're comfortable with or is quick to anger, these could be signs of future instability.

Taurus (April 20 - May 20): Stubbornness and Possessiveness

Taurus is known for their loyalty and stability, but they can also be incredibly stubborn. Once they've made up their mind, it's hard to change it. If your Taurus partner refuses to compromise or always insists on getting their way, that could signal an unwillingness to adapt to your needs. Another red flag is their possessiveness. While Taurus loves security, this can sometimes translate into jealousy and controlling behavior. If they seem overly protective or suspicious, it's important to address these concerns before they escalate.

Red Flag Warning: A refusal to compromise and signs of possessiveness may indicate deeper control issues in your Taurus partner.

Gemini (May 21 - June 20): Inconsistency and Flakiness

Geminis are social butterflies who love to communicate and keep things light. However, their dual-natured personality can sometimes make them unpredictable and inconsistent. One day, they may seem completely invested, and the next, they pull away or change their mind. If your Gemini partner has trouble following through on plans, disappears for periods of time, or gives mixed signals about their feelings, take note. Their flakiness may point to a lack of emotional stability or commitment.

Red Flag Warning: Constantly shifting moods, disappearing acts, or flaky behavior are signs that your Gemini partner might struggle with emotional consistency and follow-through.

Cancer (June 21 - July 22): Over-Sensitivity and Emotional Manipulation

Cancer is a deeply emotional sign, ruled by the Moon, which makes them nurturing but also moody. While their emotional depth can be beautiful, it can also manifest as over-sensitivity. If your Cancer partner takes everything too personally or holds onto grudges, this could lead to emotional exhaustion. Another red flag is emotional manipulation—Cancer can sometimes use guilt or passive-aggressive behavior to get their way, especially when they feel insecure.

Red Flag Warning: If your Cancer partner frequently uses guilt or emotional manipulation to control the relationship, or if they are constantly offended by minor issues, this could signal emotional instability.

Leo (July 23 - August 22): Self-Centeredness and Need for Attention

Leos love the spotlight and often crave admiration. While their confidence can be attractive, one major red flag is their need to always be the center of attention. If your Leo partner seems more focused on their own needs and achievements than on the relationship, or if they demand constant validation without reciprocating, this could lead to an imbalanced dynamic. Leos can also be prone to dramatic outbursts when they feel they aren't getting the attention they deserve.

Red Flag Warning: If your Leo partner constantly demands attention and makes everything about themselves, it may indicate narcissistic tendencies that could harm the relationship.

Virgo (August 23 - September 22): Over-Critical and Perfectionistic

Virgos are analytical and detail-oriented, which can be great for problem-solving but harmful in relationships. One of the biggest red flags with Virgo is their tendency to be overly critical. If they constantly nitpick your appearance, behavior, or decisions, this could signal deeper perfectionist tendencies that are hard to satisfy. Virgos are also known for their high standards, which can lead to unrealistic expectations and dissatisfaction with anything less than perfection.

Red Flag Warning: If your Virgo partner is hypercritical or expects perfection in every aspect of the relationship, they may struggle with accepting flaws and imperfections.

Libra (September 23 - October 22): Indecisiveness and Avoidance of Conflict

Libra values balance and harmony, but their desire to keep the peace can lead to indecisiveness and avoidance of conflict. If your Libra partner consistently avoids difficult conversations or refuses to make important decisions in the relationship, this could become a significant issue over time.

Libras also tend to be people-pleasers, which can lead them to hide their true feelings or pretend everything is fine when it's not.

Red Flag Warning: If your Libra partner is overly indecisive or avoids addressing problems, they may struggle with facing conflicts and making necessary relationship choices.

Scorpio (October 23 - November 21): Jealousy and Control

Scorpio is known for its intensity, passion, and desire for deep emotional connection. However, Scorpios can also be extremely possessive and jealous. One of the most significant red flags in a Scorpio partner is their need for control, especially over your social life or personal decisions. They may demand excessive loyalty and become suspicious of even harmless interactions with others. Scorpios are also known to be secretive, which can make it difficult to build trust.

Red Flag Warning: Excessive jealousy, controlling behavior, and secrecy are clear red flags that may signal insecurity or trust issues with your Scorpio partner.

Sagittarius (November 22 - December 21): Commitment Phobia and Restlessness

Sagittarius loves freedom, adventure, and exploration, but this can sometimes translate into a fear of commitment. One major red flag in a Sagittarius partner is their tendency to shy away from serious relationships, often preferring casual flings or open-ended arrangements. They may also become restless or bored easily, seeking excitement outside the relationship. If your Sagittarius partner avoids conversations about the future or constantly talks about their next adventure without you, it may indicate that they're not ready for long-term commitment.

Red Flag Warning: If your Sagittarius partner is evasive about commitment or seems restless and unfocused in the relationship, they may struggle with settling down.

Capricorn (December 22 - January 19): Workaholism and Emotional Distance

Capricorns are ambitious and goal-oriented, which makes them hard-working but sometimes emotionally distant. A significant red flag in Capricorn partners is their tendency to prioritize work and career over relationships. If they frequently cancel plans, neglect emotional intimacy, or seem more focused on their professional goals than on building a connection, this could lead to feelings of neglect. Capricorns can also be emotionally guarded, which makes it hard for them to open up and express their true feelings.

Red Flag Warning: If your Capricorn partner is constantly working and seems emotionally unavailable, it may signal an inability to prioritize emotional intimacy.

Aquarius (January 20 - February 18): Detachment and Unpredictability

Aquarius is known for being independent, intellectual, and unconventional. However, one major red flag in Aquarius is their tendency to detach emotionally when things get too intense. If your Aquarius partner seems distant or emotionally unavailable, it's important to address this early on. They may also have unpredictable behaviors or sudden shifts in their feelings about the relationship. While they value freedom and autonomy, this can sometimes make them unreliable in emotional matters.

Red Flag Warning: If your Aquarius partner frequently detaches emotionally or exhibits unpredictable behavior, they may struggle with commitment and emotional vulnerability.

Pisces (February 19 - March 20): Escapism and Lack of Boundaries

Pisces is highly sensitive and empathetic, often deeply attuned to the emotional needs of others. However, a significant red flag with Pisces is their tendency toward escapism. If your Pisces partner avoids dealing with problems by retreating into fantasy, substance abuse, or other forms of avoidance, this could signal an inability to face reality. Additionally, Pisces may struggle with setting boundaries, often taking on too much emotional baggage from others, which can lead to co-dependent behavior.

Red Flag Warning: If your Pisces partner frequently escapes reality or struggles to set healthy boundaries, this could signal deeper emotional and psychological issues that need to be addressed.

Conclusion

While every zodiac sign has its unique strengths, it's important to recognize the red flags that may arise in relationships. By understanding the potential pitfalls of each sign, you can better navigate dating and relationships with awareness and clarity. Remember, these red flags aren't necessarily deal breakers, but they are important to acknowledge and address early on to ensure a healthy and balanced relationship.

Chapter 19

Commitment and Sex: How Each Zodiac Sign Approaches Long-Term Relationships

Long-term commitment can bring out different aspects of a zodiac sign's personality, particularly when it comes to balancing emotional intimacy and sexual needs. Understanding how each zodiac sign approaches commitment and sex can help you navigate relationships more effectively. In this chapter, we explore how each sign handles the delicate balance between the desire for lasting love and their sexual expression in committed relationships.

Aries (March 21 - April 19): Passionate and Independent

Aries approaches commitment with fiery enthusiasm, but their need for independence can sometimes clash with the stability of long-term relationships. In the bedroom, Aries thrives on passion and excitement, and they can lose interest if things become too routine. For Aries, commitment works best when they still feel free to pursue their own goals and adventures. Sexually, they value spontaneity and physical intensity. To maintain a healthy long-term relationship, Aries needs to feel that their sexual energy is met with equal enthusiasm from their partner.

Key to Balance: Keep the excitement alive and allow for independence while maintaining a strong sexual connection.

Taurus (April 20 - May 20): Loyal and Sensual

Taurus is one of the most loyal and committed signs in the zodiac, often seeking long-term relationships that provide emotional and physical security. Sexually, Taurus is sensual and enjoys the slow build of intimacy, finding pleasure in the tactile and physical aspects of love. In a committed relationship, Taurus is steadfast, but they expect loyalty and stability in return. Their approach to sex is deeply connected to emotional trust, and they seek a partner who can provide both security and physical affection.

Key to Balance: Create an atmosphere of trust and loyalty, with a focus on sensual, intimate moments.

Gemini (May 21 - June 20): Curious and Playful

Gemini craves mental stimulation and variety, which can make long-term commitment feel challenging at times. In relationships, they are playful and communicative, and they thrive when there's plenty of intellectual exchange. Sexually, Gemini is curious and enjoys experimenting with different forms of intimacy. To keep Gemini engaged in a long-term relationship, it's important to maintain an open line of communication and introduce variety into your sex life. They need both mental and physical stimulation to stay committed.

Key to Balance: Keep the relationship dynamic and exciting, with a focus on playful and communicative sexual experiences.

Cancer (June 21 - July 22): Nurturing and Emotionally Driven

Cancer values emotional intimacy and security in long-term relationships. They are nurturing and deeply committed to their partner's well-being, but they require emotional closeness to feel secure. Sexually, Cancer is tender and affectionate, and they see physical intimacy as an extension of emotional connection. For Cancer, long-term commitment means building a home together and creating a safe space for emotional vulnerability. They need a partner who is willing to reciprocate emotionally, as their sexual satisfaction is tied closely to feeling loved and appreciated.

Key to Balance: Foster emotional security and allow sex to be a deeply intimate, nurturing experience.

Leo (July 23 - August 22): Devoted and Passionate

Leos are fiercely loyal and protective in committed relationships, and they love to make their partner feel special. Sexually, Leo is passionate, and they enjoy being admired and desired by their partner. They bring a lot of energy to the bedroom and appreciate a partner who celebrates their confidence. While Leos are dedicated in long-term relationships, they also need attention and affirmation to feel valued. For Leo, commitment is about maintaining the passion and excitement while also ensuring they feel adored.

Key to Balance: Keep the passion alive by expressing admiration and ensuring that Leo feels valued both emotionally and sexually.

Virgo (August 23 - September 22): Devoted and Thoughtful

Virgo is methodical and thoughtful in long-term relationships, often focusing on how to make their partner's life better. Sexually, Virgo can be surprisingly attentive and detail-oriented, ensuring that their partner's needs are met. While they may not always be the most spontaneous in the bedroom, they are dedicated to creating a fulfilling sexual experience. In a committed relationship, Virgo seeks stability and often prefers routine, but they need to feel appreciated for their efforts. They value loyalty and consistency in both emotional and sexual aspects of the relationship.

Key to Balance: Show appreciation for Virgo's dedication and be open to experimenting within the bounds of their comfort zone.

Libra (September 23 - October 22): Romantic and Harmonious

Libra values balance and harmony in relationships, and they approach long-term commitment with a strong desire to create a peaceful and loving partnership. Sexually, Libra is sensual and romantic, enjoying physical intimacy that feels balanced and mutual. They are generous lovers who prioritize their partner's pleasure, but they also need a relationship that feels emotionally and aesthetically balanced. Libra thrives in committed relationships where both partners put in equal effort to maintain harmony, both in and out of the bedroom.

Key to Balance: Maintain balance and equality in emotional and sexual exchanges, focusing on romance and mutual satisfaction.

Scorpio (October 23 - November 21): Intense and Loyal

Scorpio is known for its intensity and passion in both emotional and sexual relationships. When they commit, they do so with deep loyalty and expect the same in return. Sexually, Scorpio is passionate and seeks a profound emotional connection through intimacy. For them, physical intimacy is an expression of trust and vulnerability, and they expect their partner to meet them at the same emotional depth. Scorpio can be possessive and may struggle with trust issues, so they need a partner who is equally committed and willing to dive deep emotionally and sexually.

Key to Balance: Build a foundation of trust and emotional depth, and allow sexual intimacy to serve as an expression of loyalty and vulnerability.

Sagittarius (November 22 - December 21): Adventurous and Freedom-Loving

Sagittarius is known for its love of freedom and adventure, which can make long-term commitment challenging. However, when Sagittarius does commit, they bring a sense of excitement and enthusiasm to the relationship. Sexually, they are adventurous and open to exploring new experiences with their partner. To keep a Sagittarius engaged in a long-term relationship, it's important to allow space for independence and exploration. They need a partner who shares their love for adventure, both emotionally and sexually.

Key to Balance: Allow for freedom and adventure, and keep the sexual relationship dynamic and exciting.

Capricorn (December 22 - January 19): Ambitious and Loyal

Capricorn approaches long-term commitment with seriousness and dedication. They are loyal and reliable partners who value stability and long-term goals. Sexually, Capricorn is often more reserved but deeply sensual once they feel secure with their partner. They prioritize building a stable foundation in a relationship before fully opening up emotionally or sexually. Capricorn needs a partner who is equally committed to the future, and they thrive in relationships that are built on trust and shared goals.

Key to Balance: Foster long-term goals and stability, allowing Capricorn to feel secure before deepening emotional and sexual intimacy.

Aquarius (January 20 - February 18): Independent and Unconventional

Aquarius values independence and intellectual connection in relationships. While they may seem emotionally detached at times, they are deeply committed to partnerships that allow for freedom and personal growth. Sexually, Aquarius is open-minded and unconventional, often interested in exploring different forms of intimacy. In a long-term relationship, they need a partner who respects their need for autonomy while also engaging them on an intellectual and emotional level. Aquarius seeks a balance between commitment and freedom, and they thrive when their partner shares their progressive views on love and sex.

Key to Balance: Respect Aquarius's need for independence and keep the relationship intellectually stimulating and sexually open-minded.

Pisces (February 19 - March 20): Compassionate and Dreamy

Pisces is deeply emotional and compassionate, often seeking a spiritual and emotional connection in long-term relationships. Sexually, Pisces is intuitive and desires intimacy that feels transcendent and emotionally fulfilling. In a committed relationship, Pisces often blurs the lines between emotional and physical connection, seeking a partner who can meet them on a soulful level. They are incredibly giving lovers but can sometimes lose themselves in the needs of their partner. To keep Pisces fulfilled in a long-term relationship, it's important to maintain a balance between emotional intimacy and physical affection.

Key to Balance: Cultivate an emotional and spiritual connection, while ensuring Pisces's emotional needs are met both in and out of the bedroom.

Conclusion

Each zodiac sign approaches long-term commitment and sexual relationships in its own unique way. Understanding how your partner's sign balances their emotional and sexual needs can help foster a more fulfilling and harmonious relationship. Whether you're dealing with an adventurous Sagittarius or a deeply emotional Cancer, recognizing how each sign navigates commitment can lead to a deeper, more satisfying connection.

Chapter 20

Turn-Ons and Turn-Offs: What Each Zodiac Sign Craves and Avoids

Understanding what arouses and repels each zodiac sign can offer deep insights into maintaining passion and intimacy in your relationships. While each person is unique, certain traits, behaviors, and approaches tend to align with the energy of their zodiac sign. In this chapter, we explore the turn-ons and turn-offs for each zodiac sign to help you ignite or maintain the spark and avoid common relationship missteps.

Aries (March 21 - April 19)

- **Turn-Ons:** Aries loves a challenge and craves excitement. They are drawn to confidence, spontaneity, and physical energy. Bold moves, quick decision-making, and a bit of healthy competition ignite their passion. Passionate, adventurous sex and trying new things are major turn-ons.

- **Turn-Offs:** Slow, indecisive behavior and overly cautious partners frustrate Aries. Clinginess and a lack of ambition can turn them off quickly. They need action, and too much overthinking or timidity will bore them.

Keep the Spark Alive: Keep things exciting, spontaneous, and full of action. Show confidence, initiate physical contact, and be adventurous in and out of the bedroom.

Taurus (April 20 - May 20)

- **Turn-Ons:** Taurus loves sensuality and comfort. They are deeply aroused by touch, scent, and other sensory pleasures. A partner who makes them feel secure and pampered, while indulging in physical intimacy, is a huge turn-on. They appreciate thoughtful gestures, such as massages, delicious food, and romantic atmospheres.

- **Turn-Offs:** Rushed intimacy, unpredictability, and instability turn Taurus off. They dislike anything that feels chaotic or lacking in comfort. Loud, aggressive behaviors or emotional inconsistency can push them away.

Keep the Spark Alive: Create a sensual, luxurious environment. Show consistency and patience, and be tactile and affectionate with Taurus.

Gemini (May 21 - June 20)

- **Turn-Ons:** Mental stimulation is key for Gemini. They love witty conversation, flirting, and partners who can keep up with their fast-paced thinking. Variety and playful banter turn them on, as does intellectual curiosity. Gemini thrives on spontaneity and fresh experiences.

- **Turn-Offs:** Predictability and routine bore Gemini quickly. They also get turned off by overly serious, rigid, or emotionally demanding partners. Stagnant energy or monotony will push them away.

Keep the Spark Alive: Keep conversations lively and flirtatious. Be flexible, open to new experiences, and maintain a playful attitude.

Cancer (June 21 - July 22)

- **Turn-Ons:** Emotional intimacy and nurturing are vital for Cancer. They are turned on by a partner who makes them feel safe, secure, and cherished. Thoughtfulness, acts of kindness, and vulnerability help Cancer open up sexually. They enjoy intimate settings that foster emotional connection.

- **Turn-Offs:** Coldness, insensitivity, or emotional detachment quickly repel Cancer. They dislike conflict, criticism, and partners who don't respect their emotions. Fast, impersonal approaches to intimacy won't work for them.

Keep the Spark Alive: Nurture Cancer emotionally and show genuine care and affection. Build emotional trust before exploring deeper physical intimacy.

Leo (July 23 - August 22)

- **Turn-Ons:** Leo thrives on attention, admiration, and compliments. They love a partner who makes them feel special and adored, both emotionally and sexually. Leos enjoy drama, passion, and grand gestures of love. Physical touch, especially in a way that makes them feel desired, is a big turn-on.

- **Turn-Offs:** Disrespect, lack of appreciation, and dismissive behavior will turn off Leo. They cannot stand being ignored or undervalued. Routine or emotionally distant partners will leave them feeling unsatisfied.

Keep the Spark Alive: Shower Leo with admiration and affection. Be generous with compliments, and keep the relationship exciting with passionate energy.

Virgo (August 23 - September 22)

- **Turn-Ons:** Virgo is aroused by precision and attentiveness. They appreciate thoughtful details, cleanliness, and a partner who is considerate of their needs. Virgo enjoys a partner who is mentally stimulating and emotionally stable. A sense of order and well-thought-out intimacy turns them on.

- **Turn-Offs:** Messiness, chaos, and inconsistency are huge turn-offs for Virgo. They dislike partners who are disorganized, impulsive, or too emotionally unpredictable. Sloppy approaches to romance and intimacy repel them.

Keep the Spark Alive: Show attention to detail and respect Virgo's need for order. Be mindful of your approach, and create thoughtful, clean, and organized moments of intimacy.

Libra (September 23 - October 22)

- **Turn-Ons:** Libra is attracted to beauty, balance, and harmony. They are aroused by intellectual conversations, elegance, and romantic gestures. A partner who is charming, diplomatic, and well-groomed will easily turn Libra on. Aesthetic experiences, such as candlelit dinners or soft music, are key.

- **Turn-Offs:** Aggression, rudeness, and imbalance are major turn-offs. Libra cannot tolerate conflict or harsh environments. They dislike partners who are argumentative, too loud, or lack tact.

Keep the Spark Alive: Maintain a peaceful, beautiful environment. Be gentle, romantic, and avoid conflict as much as possible.

Scorpio (October 23 - November 21)

- **Turn-Ons:** Scorpio is turned on by intensity, passion, and emotional depth. They crave deep, transformative connections and are highly aroused by mystery and intrigue. Scorpio enjoys a partner who can match their emotional and sexual intensity. Trust and vulnerability are crucial turn-ons.

- **Turn-Offs:** Superficiality and dishonesty will quickly repel Scorpio. They dislike partners who are emotionally closed off or afraid of intimacy. Lack of commitment or emotional depth will turn them off.

Keep the Spark Alive: Foster deep emotional bonds and maintain an air of mystery. Be honest, passionate, and ready to explore emotional and physical intimacy on a profound level.

Sagittarius (November 22 - December 21)

- **Turn-Ons:** Sagittarius is aroused by adventure, freedom, and spontaneity. They love partners who are open-minded, fun, and willing to explore new experiences. Sagittarius enjoys a sense of playfulness in the relationship and thrives on intellectual stimulation and humor.

- **Turn-Offs:** Clinginess, neediness, and routines bore Sagittarius. They dislike partners who are too restrictive or emotionally demanding. Predictability and a lack of adventure turn them off.

Keep the Spark Alive: Be open to new experiences and keep the energy light and fun. Give Sagittarius space to explore, and keep the relationship adventurous.

Capricorn (December 22 - January 19)

- **Turn-Ons:** Capricorn is attracted to stability, ambition, and reliability. They are aroused by partners who are strong, dependable, and successful. Capricorn values traditional approaches to intimacy, and they appreciate partners who are respectful and considerate of their boundaries.

- **Turn-Offs:** Flakiness, irresponsibility, and laziness turn Capricorn off. They dislike partners who are immature or lack direction. Disrespectful or overly casual behavior in romance and sex won't appeal to them.

Keep the Spark Alive: Be dependable, respectful, and ambitious. Show Capricorn that you value long-term goals and are serious about the relationship.

Aquarius (January 20 - February 18)

- **Turn-Ons:** Aquarius is turned on by uniqueness, intellectual stimulation, and independence. They love partners who think outside the box, are open to unconventional experiences, and can hold fascinating conversations. Aquarius values mental connection and appreciates innovation in the bedroom.

- **Turn-Offs:** Conformity, emotional drama, and possessiveness turn Aquarius off. They dislike partners who are overly traditional or clingy. Lack of intellectual depth or open-mindedness will drive them away.

Keep the Spark Alive: Be intellectually stimulating, open to new ideas, and give Aquarius the freedom they need. Foster a relationship that feels unconventional and exciting.

Pisces (February 19 - March 20)

- **Turn-Ons:** Pisces is aroused by romance, emotional depth, and creativity. They are highly intuitive and crave a spiritual or emotional connection with their partner. Pisces loves dreamy, intimate environments, and they are turned on by partners who show compassion and creativity in the bedroom.

- **Turn-Offs:** Harshness, insensitivity, and overly practical approaches to romance turn Pisces off. They dislike partners who are emotionally distant or lack imagination. Conflict and criticism can make them withdraw.

Keep the Spark Alive: Nurture Pisces emotionally and create romantic, intimate settings. Show sensitivity and engage their imagination through creative and tender moments of intimacy.

Conclusion

Understanding the turn-ons and turn-offs of each zodiac sign can help you build deeper, more meaningful connections with your partner. Whether you're in a new relationship or looking to reignite the passion in a long-term commitment, recognizing the unique needs and desires of each sign can ensure a satisfying, exciting, and fulfilling relationship.

ENGAGE WITH ESRA OZ

I would like to thank all of you for purchasing my book. I would love to hear from you on how you experienced the *Astrology Dating Guide*. If you are wanting to go deeper in your courageous work in dating, you can find my "Dating Funnel for Women: How to Spot Bad Boys & Filter Them Out Quickly; 100 Types of Men to Avoid" on Amazon. This is an easy-to-follow guide on identifying and avoiding the types of men who are not worth your time. It teaches a simplistic dating approach, going on multiple dates with a variety of men and filtering out the high-value one, who is offering you the solidity, maturity, and adulthood you need for life partnership.

You can also join my social media community **"Dating Funnel for Women"** on Facebook and/or Instagram. Look for tips on dating and how to create a dating funnel. I look forward to having you join me.

Dating Funnel for Women Podcast

For more tips on how to date with more intention and less stress, listen to my podcast **"Dating Funnel for Women"** on Spotify and Apple Podcast. I also offer live group coaching on a rotating schedule and 1:1 coaching. Check out the website **www.datingfunnelforwomen.com** to see when the next session begins, explore the master class, and download a dating funnel blueprint as a reference for your dating journey and follow me on Instagram **@dresraoz**.

www.datingfunnelforwomen.com

www.ingramcontent.com/pod-product-compliance
Lightning Source LLC
LaVergne TN
LVHW051421080426
835508LV00022B/3185